Cram101 Textbook Outlines to accompany:

Principles of Corporate Finance

Richard A. Brealey, Franklin Allen, Stewart C. Myers, 1st Edition

A Cram101 Inc. publication (c) 2010.

Cram101 Textbook Outlines and Cram101.com are Cram101 Inc. publications and services. All notes, highlights, reviews, and practice tests are written and prepared by Cram101, all rights reserved.

PRACTICE EXAMS.

Get all of the self-teaching practice exams for each chapter of this textbook at **www.Cram101.com** and ace the tests. Here is an example:

Chapter 1

Principles of Corporate Finance
Richard A. Brealey, Franklin Allen, Stewart C. Myers, 1st Edition,
All Material Written and Prepared by Cram101

I WANT A BETTER GRADE.   Items 1 - 50 of 100.

1 The _____ are the primary rules governing the management of a corporation in the United States and Canada, and are filed with a state or other regulatory agency. The equivalent in the United Kingdom and various other countries is Articles of Association.

A corporation"s _____ generally provide information such as:

· The corporation"s name, which has to be unique from any other corporation in that jurisdiction. As part of the corporation"s name, certain words such as "incorporated", "limited", "corporation", (or their abbreviations) or some equivalent term in countries whose language is not English, are usually required as part of the name as a "flag" to indicate to persons doing business with the organization that it is a corporation as opposed to an individual or partnership (with unlimited liability).

- ○ Articles of incorporation
- ○ Aberdeen Street
- ○ ABC analysis
- ○ Abnormal return

2 A _____ is a financial institution licensed by a government. Its primary activities include borrowing and lending money. Many other financial activities were allowed over time.

- ○ Bank
- ○ Bachelor of Accountancy
- ○ B share
- ○ Back office

3 A _____ is a body of elected or appointed members who jointly oversee the activities of a company or

---

You get a 50% discount for the online exams. Go to **Cram101.com**, click Sign Up at the top of the screen, and enter DK73DW5383 in the promo code box on the registration screen. Access to Cram101.com is $4.95 per month, cancel at any time.

With Cram101.com online, you also have access to extensive reference material.

You will nail those essays and papers. Here is an example from a Cram101 Biology text:

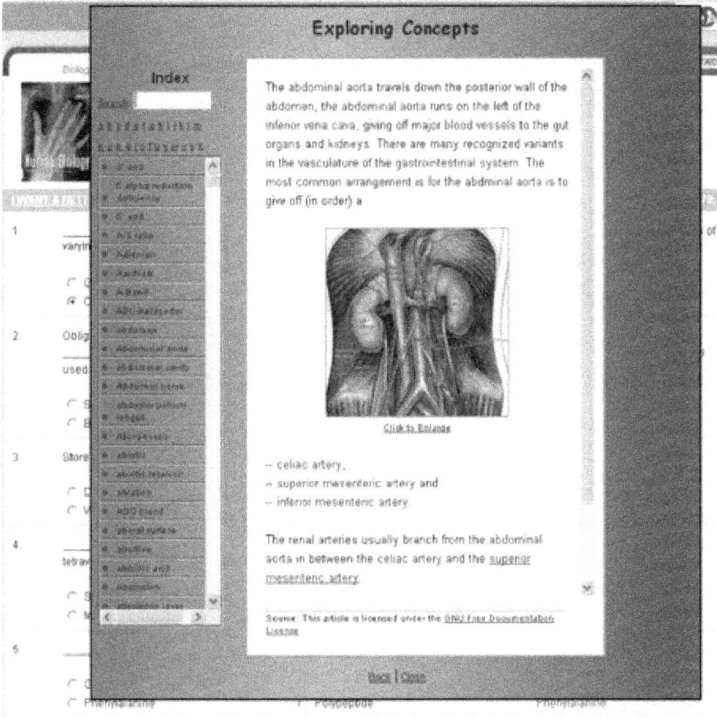

Visit **www.Cram101.com**, click Sign Up at the top of the screen, and enter DK73DW5383 in the promo code box on the registration screen. Access to www.Cram101.com is normally $9.95 per month, but because you have purchased this book, your access fee is only $4.95 per month, cancel at any time. Sign up and stop highlighting textbooks forever.

Learning System

Cram101 Textbook Outlines is a learning system. The notes in this book are the highlights of your textbook, you will never have to highlight a book again.

How to use this book. Take this book to class, it is your notebook for the lecture. The notes and highlights on the left hand side of the pages follow the outline and order of the textbook. All you have to do is follow along while your instructor presents the lecture. Circle the items emphasized in class and add other important information on the right side. With Cram101 Textbook Outlines you'll spend less time writing and more time listening. Learning becomes more efficient.

Cram101.com Online

Increase your studying efficiency by using Cram101.com's practice tests and online reference material. It is the perfect complement to Cram101 Textbook Outlines. Use self-teaching matching tests or simulate in-class testing with comprehensive multiple choice tests, or simply use Cram's true and false tests for quick review. Cram101.com even allows you to enter your in-class notes for an integrated studying format combining the textbook notes with your class notes.

Visit **www.Cram101.com**, click Sign Up at the top of the screen, and enter **DK73DW5383** in the promo code box on the registration screen. Access to www.Cram101.com is normally $9.95 per month, but because you have purchased this book, your access fee is only $4.95 per month. Sign up and stop highlighting textbooks forever.

Copyright © 2010 by Cram101, Inc. All rights reserved. "Cram101"® and "Never Highlight a Book Again!"® are registered trademarks of Cram101, Inc. ISBN(s): 9781428833258.

Principles of Corporate Finance
Richard A. Brealey, Franklin Allen, Stewart C. Myers, 1st

CONTENTS

1. Finance and the Financial Manager 2
2. Present Values, the Objectives of the Firm, and Corporate Governance 12
3. How to Calculate Present Values 24
4. Valuing Bonds 32
5. The Value of Common Stocks 40
6. Why Net Present Value Leads to Better Investment Decisions than Other Criteria 56
7. Making Investment Decisions with the Net Present Value Rule 66
8. Introduction to Risk, Return, and the Opportunity Cost of Capital 84
9. Risk and Return 92
10. Capital Budgeting and Risk 104
11. Project Analysis 118
12. Efficient Markets and Behavioral Finance 126
13. Payout Policy 144
14. Does Debt Policy Matter? 154
15. How Much Should a Firm Borrow? 162
16. Financing and Valuation 172

Chapter 1. Finance and the Financial Manager

Articles of incorporation	The Articles of incorporation are the primary rules governing the management of a corporation in the United States and Canada, and are filed with a state or other regulatory agency. The equivalent in the United Kingdom and various other countries is Articles of Association. A corporation"s Articles of incorporation generally provide information such as: · The corporation"s name, which has to be unique from any other corporation in that jurisdiction. As part of the corporation"s name, certain words such as "incorporated", "limited", "corporation", (or their abbreviations) or some equivalent term in countries whose language is not English, are usually required as part of the name as a "flag" to indicate to persons doing business with the organization that it is a corporation as opposed to an individual or partnership (with unlimited liability).
Bank	A Bank is a financial institution licensed by a government. Its primary activities include borrowing and lending money. Many other financial activities were allowed over time.
Board of directors	A Board of directors is a body of elected or appointed members who jointly oversee the activities of a company or organization. The body sometimes has a different name, such as board of trustees, board of governors, board of managers, or executive board. It is often simply referred to as "the board." A board"s activities are determined by the powers, duties, and responsibilities delegated to it or conferred on it by an authority outside itself.
Partnership	Partnerships may be formed in the legal forms of General Partnership (Offene Handelsgesellschaft, OHG) or Limited Partnership (Kommanditgesellschaft, KG). A Partnership can be formed by only one person. In the OHG, all partners are fully liable for the Partnership"s debts, whereas in the KG there are general partners with unlimited liability and limited partners whose liability is restricted to their fixed contributions to the Partnership.
Shareholder	A mutual Shareholder or stockholder is an individual or company (including a corporation) that legally owns one or more shares of stock in a joint stock company. A company"s Shareholders collectively own that company. Thus, the typical goal of such companies is to enhance Shareholder value.
Proprietorship	A sole Proprietorship also known as a sole trader. All assets of the business are owned by the proprietor and all debts of the business are his debts and he must pay them from his personal resources.
Liability	In financial accounting, a liability is defined as an obligation of an entity arising from past transactions or events, the settlement of which may result in the transfer or use of assets, provision of services or other yielding of economic benefits in the future. · All type of borrowing from persons or banks for improving a business or person income which is payable during short or long time. · They embody a duty or responsibility to others that entails settlement by future transfer or use of assets, provision of services or other yielding of economic benefits, at a specified or determinable date, on occurrence of a specified event, or on demand; · The duty or responsibility obligates the entity leaving it little or no discretion to avoid it; and, · The transaction or event obligating the entity has already occurred.

Chapter 1. Finance and the Financial Manager

	Liabilities in financial accounting need not be legally enforceable; but can be based on equitable obligations or constructive obligations. An equitable obligation is a duty based on ethical or moral considerations.
Restructuring	restructuring is the corporate management term for the act of reorganizing the legal, ownership, operational, or better organized for its present needs. Alternate reasons f include a change of ownership or ownership structure, demerger, or a response to a crisis or major change in the business such as bankruptcy, repositioning, or buyout. restructuring may also be described as corporate restructuring, debt restructuring and financial restructuring.
Capital budgeting	Capital budgeting (or investment appraisal) is the planning process used to determine whether a firm"s long term investments such as new machinery, replacement machinery, new plants, new products, and research development projects are worth pursuing. It is budget for major capital, or investment, expenditures. Many formal methods are used in Capital budgeting, including the techniques such as · Accounting rate of return · Net present value · Profitability index · Internal rate of return · Modified Internal Rate of Return · Equivalent annuity These methods use the incremental cash flows from each potential investment, or project Techniques based on accounting earnings and accounting rules are sometimes used - though economists consider this to be improper - such as the accounting rate of return, and "return on investment." Simplified and hybrid methods are used as well, such as payback period and discounted payback period. Each potential project"s value should be estimated using a discounted cash flow (DCF) valuation, to find its net present value (NPV).
Capital market	A Capital market is a market for securities (both debt and equity), where business enterprises (companies) and governments can raise long-term funds. It is defined as a market in which money is lent for periods longer than a year, as the raising of short-term funds takes place on other markets (e.g., the money market). The Capital market includes the stock market (equity securities) and the bond market (debt).
Asset	In business and accounting, Assets are economic resources owned by business or company. Anything tangible or intangible that one possesses, usually considered as applicable to the payment of one"s debts is considered an Asset. Simplistically stated, Assets are things of value that can be readily converted into cash (although cash itself is also considered an Asset).
Finance	Finance is the science of funds management. The general areas of Finance are business Finance, personal Finance, and public Finance. Finance includes saving money and often includes lending money.
Securities	A security is a fungible, negotiable instrument representing financial value. Securities are broadly categorized into debt Securities (such as banknotes, bonds and debentures); equity Securities, e.g., common stocks; and derivative contracts, such as forwards, futures, options and swaps. The company or other entity issuing the security is called the issuer.

Chapter 1. Finance and the Financial Manager

Chapter 1. Finance and the Financial Manager

Investment	Investment or investing is a term with several closely-related meanings in business management, finance and economics, related to saving or deferring consumption. Investing is the active redirection of resources: from being consumed today, to creating benefits in the future; the use of assets to earn income or profit. An Investment is a choice by an individual or an organization such as a pension fund, after at least some careful analysis or thought, to place or lend money in a vehicle (e.g. property, stock securities, bonds) that has sufficiently low risk and provides the possibility of generating returns over a period of time.
Investment decisions	Investment decisions are made by investors and investment managers. Investors commonly perform investment analysis by making use of fundamental analysis, technical analysis and gut feel. Investment decisions are often supported by decision tools.
Short-run	In economics, the concept of the short-run refers to the decision-making time frame of a firm in which at least one factor of production is fixed. Costs which are fixed in the short-run have no impact on a firms decisions. For example a firm can raise output by increasing the amount of labour through overtime. A generic firm can make three changes in the short-run: · Increase production · Decrease production · Shut down In the short-run, a profit maximizing firm will: · Increase production if marginal cost is less than price; · Decrease production if marginal cost is greater than price; · Continue producing if average variable cost is less than price, even if average total cost is greater than price; · Shut down if average variable cost is greater than price.
Debt	Debt is that which is owed; usually referencing assets owed, but the term can also cover moral obligations and other interactions not requiring money. In the case of assets, Debt is a means of using future purchasing power in the present before a summation has been earned. Some companies and corporations use Debt as a part of their overall corporate finance strategy.
Return	Returns .
Contract	In common-law systems, the five key requirements for the creation of a Contract are: 1. offer and acceptance (agreement) 2. consideration 3. an intention to create legal relations 4. legal capacity 5. formalities In civil-law systems, the concept of consideration is not central. In addition, for some Contracts formalities must be complied with under what is sometimes called a statute of frauds. One of the most famous cases on forming a Contract is Carlill v. Carbolic Smoke Ball Company, decided in nineteenth-century England.

Chapter 1. Finance and the Financial Manager

Liquidity	Market liquidity is a business, economics or investment term that refers to an asset"s ability to be easily converted through an act of buying or selling without causing a significant movement in the price and with minimum loss of value. Money, or cash on hand, is the most liquid asset. An act of exchange of a less liquid asset with a more liquid asset is called liquidation.
Financial markets	In economics, a financial market is a mechanism that allows people to easily buy and sell (trade) financial securities (such as stocks and bonds), commodities (such as precious metals or agricultural goods), and other fungible items of value at low transaction costs and at prices that reflect the efficient-market hypothesis.
	Financial markets have evolved significantly over several hundred years and are undergoing constant innovation to improve liquidity.
	Both general markets (where many commodities are traded) and specialized markets (where only one commodity is traded) exist.
Chief brand officer	A Chief brand officer is a relatively new executive level position at a corporation, company, organization, typically reporting directly to the CEO or board of directors. The Chief brand officer is responsible for a brand"s image, experience, and promise, and propagating it throughout all aspects of the company. The brand officer oversees marketing, advertising, design, public relations and customer service departments. The brand equity of a company is seen as becoming increasingly dependent on the role of a Chief brand officer.
	Companies that currently employ a Chief brand officer include: · Srinivas Kumar, Baskin-Robbins Worldwide · Michael Keller, Dairy Queen · Will Kussell, Dunkin" Brands, Inc. · Trey Hall, Boston Market Corporation · Allen Schiffenbaure, G 2 Marketing Group · Alan Bergstrom, Storyminers Inc. · Brian Igoe, Metabolix, Inc. · Phil Mcaveety, Luxury Collection · Mark I. McCallum, Brown-Forman Corporation · Phil McAveety, Starwood Hotels ' Resorts Worldwide, Inc. · Danny Meisenheimer, Souper Salad, Inc
Principal-agent problem	In political science and economics, the principal-agent problem or agency dilemma treats the difficulties that arise under conditions of incomplete and asymmetric information when a principal hires an agent, such as the problem that the two may not have the same interests, while the principal is, presumably, hiring the agent to pursue the interests of the former.
	Various mechanisms may be used to try to align the interests of the agent in solidarity with those of the principal, such as piece rates/commissions, profit sharing, efficiency wages, performance measurement (including financial statements), the agent posting a bond, or fear of firing. The principal-agent problem is found in most employer/employee relationships, for example, when stockholders hire top executives of corporations.
Budget	The Budget of a government is a summary or plan of the intended revenues and expenditures of that government. The United States federal Budget is prepared by the Office of Management and Budget, and submitted to Congress for consideration. Invariably, Congress makes many and substantial changes.

Chapter 1. Finance and the Financial Manager

Cost	In business, retail, and accounting, a cost is the value of money that has been used up to produce something, and hence is not available for use anymore. In economics, a cost is an alternative that is given up as a result of a decision. In business, the cost may be one of acquisition, in which case the amount of money expended to acquire it is counted as cost.
Interest	In the Renaissance era, greater mobility of people facilitated an increase in commerce and the appearance of appropriate conditions for entrepreneurs to start new, lucrative businesses. Given that borrowed money was no longer strictly for consumption but for production as well, Interest was no longer viewed in the same manner. The School of Salamanca elaborated on various reasons that justified the charging of Interest: the person who received a loan benefited, and one could consider Interest as a premium paid for the risk taken by the loaning party.
Equivalent annual cost	In finance the Equivalent annual cost is the cost per year of owning and operating an asset over its entire lifespan.
	Equivalent annual cost is often used as a decision making tool in capital budgeting when comparing investment projects of unequal lifespans. For example if project A has an expected lifetime of 7 years, and project B has an expected lifetime of 11 years it would be improper to simply compare the net present values (NPVs) of the two projects, unless neither project could be repeated.
Mortgage	A mortgage is the transfer of an interest in property (or the equivalent in law - a charge) to a lender as a security for a debt - usually a loan of money. While a mortgage in itself is not a debt, it is the lender"s security for a debt. It is a transfer of an interest in land (or the equivalent) from the owner to the mortgage lender, on the condition that this interest will be returned to the owner when the terms of the mortgage have been satisfied or performed.

Chapter 2. Present Values, the Objectives of the Firm, and Corporate Governance

Future	Futures may mean: · Futures contract, a tradable financial contract · Futures exchange, a financial market where Futures contracts are traded · Futures (magazine), an American finance magazine · Futures studies, multidisciplinary studies of patterns to determine the likelihood of Future trends · Futures (journal), an international Futures studies journal · Futures (album), a 2004 release by Jimmy Eat World · "Futures" (song), a single from the above album · Futures and promises, computer programming objects that act as proxies for results that are not yet determined · Futures tournaments, minor professional tennis events .
Future value	Future value measures the nominal future sum of money that a given sum of money is "worth" at a specified time in the future assuming a certain interest rate, rate of return; it is the present value multiplied by the accumulation function. The value does not include corrections for inflation or other factors that affect the true value of money in the future. This is used in time value of money calculations.
Net present value	Net present value or net present worth (NPW) is defined as the total present value (PV) of a time series of cash flows. It is a standard method for using the time value of money to appraise long-term projects. Used for capital budgeting, and widely throughout economics, it measures the excess or shortfall of cash flows, in present value terms, once financing charges are met.
Present value	Present value is the value on a given date of a future payment or series of future payments, discounted to reflect the time value of money and other factors such as investment risk. Present value calculations are widely used in business and economics to provide a means to compare cash flows at different times on a meaningful "like to like" basis. If offered a choice between $100 today or $100 in one year, a rational person will choose $100 today.
Time value of money	The Time value of money is the value of money figuring in a given amount of interest earned over a given amount of time. For example, 100 dollars of today"s money invested for one year and earning 5 percent interest will be worth 105 dollars after one year. Therefore, 100 dollars paid now or 105 dollars paid exactly one year from now both have the same value to the recipient assuming 5 percent interest; using Time value of money terminology, 100 dollars invested for one year at 5 percent interest has a future value of 105 dollars.
Cost	In business, retail, and accounting, a cost is the value of money that has been used up to produce something, and hence is not available for use anymore. In economics, a cost is an alternative that is given up as a result of a decision. In business, the cost may be one of acquisition, in which case the amount of money expended to acquire it is counted as cost.

Chapter 2. Present Values, the Objectives of the Firm, and Corporate Governance

Cost of capital	In business and finance, the cost of capital is the cost of obtaining funds for, or, conversely, the required return necessary to meet its cost of financing a capital budgeting project. Said another way, it is "the minimum return that a company should make on its own investments, to earn the cash flow out of which investors can be paid their return." cost of capital encompasses the two fundamental sources of financing: the cost of debt (including bonds and loans) and the cost of equity. Capital (money) used for funding a business should earn returns for the capital providers who risk their capital.
Discount rate	The Discount rate is an interest rate a central bank charges depository institutions that borrow reserves from it. The term Discount rate has two meanings: · the same as interest rate; the term "discount" does not refer to the meaning of the word, but to the purpose of using the quantity, such as computations of present value, e.g. net present value or discounted cash flow · the annual effective Discount rate, which is the annual interest divided by the capital including that interest; this rate is lower than the interest rate; it corresponds to using the value after a year as the nominal value, and seeing the initial value as the nominal value minus a discount; it is used for Treasury Bills and similar financial instruments The annual effective Discount rate is the annual interest divided by the capital including that interest, which is the interest rate divided by 100% plus the interest rate. It is the annual discount factor to be applied to the future cash flow, to find the discount, subtracted from a future value to find the value one year earlier. For example, suppose there is a government bond that sells for $95 and pays $100 in a year"s time.
Equivalent annual cost	In finance the Equivalent annual cost is the cost per year of owning and operating an asset over its entire lifespan. Equivalent annual cost is often used as a decision making tool in capital budgeting when comparing investment projects of unequal lifespans. For example if project A has an expected lifetime of 7 years, and project B has an expected lifetime of 11 years it would be improper to simply compare the net present values (NPVs) of the two projects, unless neither project could be repeated.
Monte Carlo methods	Monte Carlo methods are a class of computational algorithms that rely on repeated random sampling to compute their results. Monte Carlo methods are often used when simulating physical and mathematical systems. Because of their reliance on repeated computation of random or pseudo-random numbers, Monte Carlo methods are most suited to calculation by a computer.
Opportunity cost	Opportunity cost or economic opportunity loss is the value of the next best alternative forgone as the result of making a decision. Opportunity cost analysis is an important part of a company"s decision-making processes but is not treated as an actual cost in any financial statement. The next best thing that a person can engage in is referred to as the Opportunity cost of doing the best thing and ignoring the next best thing to be done.
Opportunity cost of capital	The opportunity cost of capital is the expected return forgone by bypassing of other potential investment activities for a given capital. It is a rate of return that investors could earn in financial markets. .
Rate of return	Yield is the compound Rate of return that includes the effect of reinvesting interest or dividends. To the right is an example of a stock investment of one share purchased at the beginning of the year for $100.

Chapter 2. Present Values, the Objectives of the Firm, and Corporate Governance

Chapter 2. Present Values, the Objectives of the Firm, and Corporate Governance

· The quarterly dividend is reinvested at the quarter-end stock price.
· The number of shares purchased each quarter = ($ Dividend)/($ Stock Price).
· The final investment value of $103.02 is a 3.02% Yield on the initial investment of $100. This is the compound yield, and this return can be considered to be the return on the investment of $100.
To calculate the Rate of return, the investor includes the reinvested dividends in the total investment. The investor received a total of $4.06 in dividends over the year, all of which were reinvested, so the investment amount increased by $4.06.

· Total Investment = Cost Basis = $100 + $4.06 = $104.06.
· Capital gain/loss = $103.02 - $104.06 = -$1.04 (a capital loss)
· ($4.06 dividends - $1.04 capital loss) / $104.06 total investment = 2.9% ROI

The disadvantage of this ROI calculation is that it does not take into account the fact that not all the money was invested during the entire year (the dividend reinvestments occurred throughout the year).

Mortgage	A mortgage is the transfer of an interest in property (or the equivalent in law - a charge) to a lender as a security for a debt - usually a loan of money. While a mortgage in itself is not a debt, it is the lender"s security for a debt. It is a transfer of an interest in land (or the equivalent) from the owner to the mortgage lender, on the condition that this interest will be returned to the owner when the terms of the mortgage have been satisfied or performed.
Capital market	A Capital market is a market for securities (both debt and equity), where business enterprises (companies) and governments can raise long-term funds. It is defined as a market in which money is lent for periods longer than a year, as the raising of short-term funds takes place on other markets (e.g., the money market). The Capital market includes the stock market (equity securities) and the bond market (debt).
Fixed tax	A Fixed tax is a lump sum tax that is not measured as a percentage of the tax base (income, wealth). Fixed taxes like a poll tax or sin tax are often considered regressive, but could have progressive effects if applied to luxury goods and services.
	Since citizens share common roads, military protection, policing, and other government services, some argue that citizens should pay the same amount for basic infrastructure.
Shareholder	A mutual Shareholder or stockholder is an individual or company (including a corporation) that legally owns one or more shares of stock in a joint stock company. A company"s Shareholders collectively own that company. Thus, the typical goal of such companies is to enhance Shareholder value.
Profit maximisation	In economics, profit maximisation is the process by which a firm determines the price and output level that returns the greatest profit. There are several approaches to this problem. The total revenue--total cost method relies on the fact that profit equals revenue minus cost, and the marginal revenue--marginal cost method is based on the fact that total profit in a perfectly competitive market reaches its maximum point where marginal revenue equals marginal cost.

Chapter 2. Present Values, the Objectives of the Firm, and Corporate Governance

Restructuring	restructuring is the corporate management term for the act of reorganizing the legal, ownership, operational, or better organized for its present needs. Alternate reasons f include a change of ownership or ownership structure, demerger, or a response to a crisis or major change in the business such as bankruptcy, repositioning, or buyout. restructuring may also be described as corporate restructuring, debt restructuring and financial restructuring.
Board of directors	A Board of directors is a body of elected or appointed members who jointly oversee the activities of a company or organization. The body sometimes has a different name, such as board of trustees, board of governors, board of managers, or executive board. It is often simply referred to as "the board." A board"s activities are determined by the powers, duties, and responsibilities delegated to it or conferred on it by an authority outside itself.
Corporate governance	Corporate governance is the set of processes, customs, policies, laws, and institutions affecting the way a corporation (or company) is directed, administered or controlled. Corporate governance also includes the relationships among the many stakeholders involved and the goals for which the corporation is governed. The principal stakeholders are the shareholders/members, management, and the board of directors.
Proxy fight	A proxy fight or proxy battle is an event that may occur when a corporation"s stockholders develop opposition to some aspect of the corporate governance, often focusing on directorial and management positions. Corporate activists may attempt to persuade shareholders to use their proxy votes (i.e. votes by one individual or institution as the authorized representative of another) to install new management for any of a variety of reasons. In a proxy fight, incumbent directors and management have the odds stacked in their favor over those trying to force the corporate change.
Takeover	A reverse Takeover is a type of Takeover where a private company acquires a public company. This is usually done at the instigation of the larger, private company, the purpose being for the private company to effectively float itself while avoiding some of the expense and time involved in a conventional IPO. However, under AIM rules, a reverse take-over is an acquisition or acquisitions in a twelve month period which for an AIM company would: · exceed 100% in any of the class tests; or · result in a fundamental change in its business, board or voting control; or · in the case of an investing company, depart substantially from the investing strategy stated in its admission document or, where no admission document was produced on admission, depart substantially from the investing strategy stated in its pre-admission announcement or, depart substantially from the investing strategy Often a company acquiring another pays a specified amount for it. This money can be raised in a number of ways. Although the company may have sufficient funds available in its account, this is unusual.
Efficient-market hypothesis	In finance, the Efficient-market hypothesis (EMH) asserts that financial markets are "informationally efficient", stocks, bonds, or property) already reflect all known information, and instantly change to reflect new information. Therefore, according to theory, it is impossible to consistently outperform the market by using any information that the market already knows, except through luck. Information or news in the EMH is defined as anything that may affect prices that is unknowable in the present and thus appears randomly in the future.

Chapter 2. Present Values, the Objectives of the Firm, and Corporate Governance

Chapter 2. Present Values, the Objectives of the Firm, and Corporate Governance

Interest	In the Renaissance era, greater mobility of people facilitated an increase in commerce and the appearance of appropriate conditions for entrepreneurs to start new, lucrative businesses. Given that borrowed money was no longer strictly for consumption but for production as well, Interest was no longer viewed in the same manner. The School of Salamanca elaborated on various reasons that justified the charging of Interest: the person who received a loan benefited, and one could consider Interest as a premium paid for the risk taken by the loaning party.
Principal-agent problem	In political science and economics, the principal-agent problem or agency dilemma treats the difficulties that arise under conditions of incomplete and asymmetric information when a principal hires an agent, such as the problem that the two may not have the same interests, while the principal is, presumably, hiring the agent to pursue the interests of the former.
	Various mechanisms may be used to try to align the interests of the agent in solidarity with those of the principal, such as piece rates/commissions, profit sharing, efficiency wages, performance measurement (including financial statements), the agent posting a bond, or fear of firing. The principal-agent problem is found in most employer/employee relationships, for example, when stockholders hire top executives of corporations.
Best interests	best interests of the child is the doctrine used by most courts to determine a wide range of issues relating to the well-being of children. The most important of these issues concern questions that arise upon the divorce or separation of the children"s parents: With whom will the children live?; How much contact will the parents, legal guardian, or other parties be allowed (or required) to have?; and To whom and by whom will child support be paid and in what amount?
	The use of the best interests doctrine represented a 20th century shift in public policy. The best interests doctrine is an aspect of parens patriae, and in the United States it has replaced the tender years doctrine, which rested on the basis that children are not resilient and almost any change in a child"s living situation would be detrimental to their well-being.
Bank	A Bank is a financial institution licensed by a government. Its primary activities include borrowing and lending money. Many other financial activities were allowed over time.
Mutual fund	A Mutual fund is a professionally managed type of collective investment scheme that pools money from many investors and invests it in stocks, bonds, short-term money market instruments, and/or other securities. The Mutual fund will have a fund manager that trades the pooled money on a regular basis. The net proceeds or losses are then typically distributed to the investors annually.
Return	Returns .
Chief executive officer	A Chief executive officer or chief executive is one of the highest-ranking corporate officers (executives) or administrators in charge of total management. An individual selected as president and Chief executive officer of a corporation, company, organization, or agency, reports to the board of directors.
	It is the responsibility of the Chief executive officer to align the company, internally and externally, with his or her strategic vision.
Irrational exuberance	"Irrational Exuberance" is a phrase used by the then Federal Reserve Board Chairman, Alan Greenspan, in a speech given at the American Enterprise Institute during the stock market boom of the 1990s. The phrase was a warning that the market might be somewhat overvalued.

Chapter 2. Present Values, the Objectives of the Firm, and Corporate Governance

Chapter 2. Present Values, the Objectives of the Firm, and Corporate Governance

Greenspan"s comment was made on December 5, 1996 (emphasis added in excerpt):

The prescience of the short comment--not repeated by Greenspan since--within a rather dry and complex speech would not normally have been so memorable; however, it was followed by immediate slumps in stock markets worldwide, provoking a strong reaction in financial circles and making its way into colloquial speech.

Sarbanes-Oxley Act

The Sarbanes-Oxley Act of 2002 (Pub.L. 107-204, 116 Stat. 745, enacted July 30, 2002), also known as the "Public Company Accounting Reform and Investor Protection Act" (in the Senate) and "Corporate and Auditing Accountability and Responsibility Act" (in the House) and commonly called Sarbanes-Oxley, Sarbox or SOX, is a United States federal law enacted on July 30, 2002, as a reaction to a number of major corporate and accounting scandals including those affecting Enron, Tyco International, Adelphia, Peregrine Systems and WorldCom. These scandals, which cost investors billions of dollars when the share prices of affected companies collapsed, shook public confidence in the nation"s securities markets. Named after sponsors U.S. Senator Paul Sarbanes (D-MD) and U.S. Representative Michael G. Oxley (R-OH), the act was approved by the House by a vote of 423-3 and by the Senate 99-0. President George W. Bush signed it into law, stating it included "the most far-reaching reforms of American business practices since the time of Franklin D. Roosevelt."

The legislation set new or enhanced standards for all U.S. public company boards, management and public accounting firms.

Sarbanes-Oxley Act of 2002

The Sarbanes-Oxley Act of 2002 (Pub.L. 107-204, 116 Stat. 745, enacted July 30, 2002), also known as the "Public Company Accounting Reform and Investor Protection Act" (in the Senate) and "Corporate and Auditing Accountability and Responsibility Act" (in the House) and commonly called Sarbanes-Oxley, Sarbox or SOX, is a United States federal law enacted on July 30, 2002, as a reaction to a number of major corporate and accounting scandals including those affecting Enron, Tyco International, Adelphia, Peregrine Systems and WorldCom. These scandals, which cost investors billions of dollars when the share prices of affected companies collapsed, shook public confidence in the nation"s securities markets. Named after sponsors U.S. Senator Paul Sarbanes (D-MD) and U.S. Representative Michael G. Oxley (R-OH), the act was approved by the House by a vote of 423-3 and by the Senate 99-0. President George W. Bush signed it into law, stating it included "the most far-reaching reforms of American business practices since the time of Franklin D. Roosevelt."

The legislation set new or enhanced standards for all U.S. public company boards, management and public accounting firms.

Acceptance

Notions of acceptance are prominent in many faiths and meditation practices. For example, Buddhism"s first noble truth, "All life is suffering", invites people to accept that suffering is a natural part of life. The term "Kabbalah" means literally acceptance.

Chapter 3. How to Calculate Present Values

Equivalent annual cost	In finance the Equivalent annual cost is the cost per year of owning and operating an asset over its entire lifespan.
	Equivalent annual cost is often used as a decision making tool in capital budgeting when comparing investment projects of unequal lifespans. For example if project A has an expected lifetime of 7 years, and project B has an expected lifetime of 11 years it would be improper to simply compare the net present values (NPVs) of the two projects, unless neither project could be repeated.
Net present value	Net present value or net present worth (NPW) is defined as the total present value (PV) of a time series of cash flows. It is a standard method for using the time value of money to appraise long-term projects. Used for capital budgeting, and widely throughout economics, it measures the excess or shortfall of cash flows, in present value terms, once financing charges are met.
Performance measurement	Performance measurement is the process whereby an organization establishes the parameters within which programs, investments, and acquisitions are reaching the desired results. Performance Reference Model of the Federal Enterprise Architecture, 2005.
	This process of measuring performance often requires the use of statistical evidence to determine progress toward specific defined organizational objectives.
	There are many types of measurements.
Asset	In business and accounting, Assets are economic resources owned by business or company. Anything tangible or intangible that one possesses, usually considered as applicable to the payment of one"s debts is considered an Asset. Simplistically stated, Assets are things of value that can be readily converted into cash (although cash itself is also considered an Asset).
Discount rate	The Discount rate is an interest rate a central bank charges depository institutions that borrow reserves from it.
	The term Discount rate has two meanings:
	· the same as interest rate; the term "discount" does not refer to the meaning of the word, but to the purpose of using the quantity, such as computations of present value, e.g. net present value or discounted cash flow
	· the annual effective Discount rate, which is the annual interest divided by the capital including that interest; this rate is lower than the interest rate; it corresponds to using the value after a year as the nominal value, and seeing the initial value as the nominal value minus a discount; it is used for Treasury Bills and similar financial instruments
	The annual effective Discount rate is the annual interest divided by the capital including that interest, which is the interest rate divided by 100% plus the interest rate. It is the annual discount factor to be applied to the future cash flow, to find the discount, subtracted from a future value to find the value one year earlier.
	For example, suppose there is a government bond that sells for $95 and pays $100 in a year"s time.
Incentive	In economics and sociology, an incentive is any factor (financial or non-financial) that enables or motivates a particular course of action, the study of incentive structures is central to the study of all economic activity (both in terms of individual decision-making and in terms of co-operation and competition within a larger institutional structure).
Cash flow	Cash flow refers to the movement of cash into or out of a business, a project, finite period of time. Measurement of Cash flow can be used

Chapter 3. How to Calculate Present Values

	· to determine a project''s rate of return or value. The time of Cash flows into and out of projects are used as inputs in financial models such as internal rate of return, and net present value. · to determine problems with a business''s liquidity.
Discounted cash flow	In finance, the Discounted cash flow approach describes a method of valuing a project, company, that reflects the risk of the cashflows.
Adjustment	Adjustment means regulating, adapting or settling in a variety of contexts: Adjustment has several meanings; many relate to insurance, contracts, or the resolution of disputes. In Engineering, Mathematics and Geodesy, Adjustment means the optimal parameter estimation of a mathematical model so as to best fit a data set. The most important method is the least squares Adjustment, found by Carl Friedrich Gauss.
Financial statements	financial statements (or financial reports) are formal records of the financial activities of a business, person, including United Kingdom company law, financial statements are often referred to as accounts, although the term financial statements is also used, particularly by accountants. financial statements provide an overview of a business or person''s financial condition in both short and long term.
Arbitrage	In economics and finance, Arbitrage is the practice of taking advantage of a price differential between two or more markets: striking a combination of matching deals that capitalize upon the imbalance, the profit being the difference between the market prices. When used by academics, an Arbitrage is a transaction that involves no negative cash flow at any probabilistic or temporal state and a positive cash flow in at least one state; in simple terms, a risk-free profit. A person who engages in Arbitrage is called an Arbitrageur--such as a bank or brokerage firm.
Yield curve	In finance, the yield curve is the relation between the interest rate (or cost of borrowing) and the time to maturity of the debt for a given borrower in a given currency. For example, the U.S. dollar interest rates paid on U.S. Treasury securities for various maturities are closely watched by many traders, and are commonly plotted on a graph such as the one on the right which is informally called "the yield curve." More formal mathematical descriptions of this relation are often called the term structure of interest rates. The yield of a debt instrument is the overall rate of return available on the investment.
Common stock	Common stock is a form of corporate equity ownership, a type of security. It is called "common" to distinguish it from preferred stock. In the event of bankruptcy, Common stock investors receive their funds after preferred stock holders, bondholders, creditors, etc.
Interest	In the Renaissance era, greater mobility of people facilitated an increase in commerce and the appearance of appropriate conditions for entrepreneurs to start new, lucrative businesses. Given that borrowed money was no longer strictly for consumption but for production as well, Interest was no longer viewed in the same manner. The School of Salamanca elaborated on various reasons that justified the charging of Interest: the person who received a loan benefited, and one could consider Interest as a premium paid for the risk taken by the loaning party.

Chapter 3. How to Calculate Present Values

Interest rates	An interest rate is the price a borrower pays for the use of money they do not own, for instance a small company might borrow from a bank to kick start their business, and the return a lender receives for deferring the use of funds, by lending it to the borrower. Interest rates are normally expressed as a percentage rate over the period of one year.
	Interest rates targets are also a vital tool of monetary policy and are used to control variables like investment, inflation, and unemployment.
Valuation	In finance, valuation is the process of estimating the potential market value of a financial asset or liability. valuations can be done on assets (for example, investments in marketable securities such as stocks, options, business enterprises, or intangible assets such as patents and trademarks) or on liabilities (e.g., Bonds issued by a company). valuations are required in many contexts including investment analysis, capital budgeting, merger and acquisition transactions, financial reporting, taxable events to determine the proper tax liability, and in litigation.
	valuation of financial assets is done using one or more of these types of models:
	· Discounted Cash Flows determine the value by estimating the expected future earnings from owning the asset discounted to their present value.
	· Relative value models determine the value based on the market prices of similar assets.
	· Option pricing models are used for certain types of financial assets (e.g., warrants, put options, call options, employee stock options, investments with embedded options such as a callable bond) and are a complex present value model.
Law of one price	The law of one price is an economic law stated as: "In an efficient market all identical goods must have only one price." The law of one price relates to the outcome of free trade and globalization. It is the theory that some day all areas of the world will make the same amount of money as every other part of the world for equal work/product quality.
	The intuition for this law is that all sellers will flock to the highest prevailing price, and all buyers to the lowest current market price.
Monte Carlo methods	Monte Carlo methods are a class of computational algorithms that rely on repeated random sampling to compute their results. Monte Carlo methods are often used when simulating physical and mathematical systems. Because of their reliance on repeated computation of random or pseudo-random numbers, Monte Carlo methods are most suited to calculation by a computer.
Forecasting	forecasting is the process of estimation in unknown situations. Prediction is a similar, but more general term. Both can refer to estimation of time series, cross-sectional or longitudinal data.
Amortizing loan	In banking and finance, an Amortizing loan is a loan where the principal of the loan is paid down over the life of the loan, according to some amortization schedule, typically through equal payments.
	Similarly, an amortizing bond is a bond that repays part of the principal (face value) along with the coupon payments. Compare with a sinking fund, which amortizes the total debt outstanding by repurchasing some bonds.
Mortgage	A mortgage is the transfer of an interest in property (or the equivalent in law - a charge) to a lender as a security for a debt - usually a loan of money. While a mortgage in itself is not a debt, it is the lender"s security for a debt. It is a transfer of an interest in land (or the equivalent) from the owner to the mortgage lender, on the condition that this interest will be returned to the owner when the terms of the mortgage have been satisfied or performed.
Future	Futures may mean:

Chapter 3. How to Calculate Present Values

Chapter 3. How to Calculate Present Values

	· Futures contract, a tradable financial contract
	· Futures exchange, a financial market where Futures contracts are traded
	· Futures (magazine), an American finance magazine
	· Futures studies, multidisciplinary studies of patterns to determine the likelihood of Future trends
	· Futures (journal), an international Futures studies journal
	· Futures (album), a 2004 release by Jimmy Eat World
	· "Futures" (song), a single from the above album
	· Futures and promises, computer programming objects that act as proxies for results that are not yet determined
	· Futures tournaments, minor professional tennis events .
Future value	Future value measures the nominal future sum of money that a given sum of money is "worth" at a specified time in the future assuming a certain interest rate, rate of return; it is the present value multiplied by the accumulation function. The value does not include corrections for inflation or other factors that affect the true value of money in the future. This is used in time value of money calculations.
Annual percentage of rate	The terms annual percentage of rate (APR), nominal APR, and effective APR (EAR) describe the interest rate for a whole year (annualized), rather than just a monthly fee/rate, as applied on a loan, mortgage, credit card, etc. It is a finance charge expressed as an annual rate. Those terms have formal, legal definitions in some countries or legal jurisdictions, but in general: · The nominal APR is the simple-interest rate (for a year). · The effective APR is the fee+compound interest rate (calculated across a year). The nominal APR is calculated as: the rate, for a payment period, multiplied by the number of payment periods in a year. However, the exact legal definition of "effective APR", or EAR in short, can vary greatly in each jurisdiction, depending on the type of fees included, such as participation fees, loan origination fees, monthly service charges, or late fees.
Compound interest	Compound interest arises when interest is added to the principal, so that from that moment on, the interest that has been added also itself earns interest. This addition of interest to the principal is called compounding (i.e. the interest is compounded). A loan, for example, may have its interest compounded every month: in this case, a loan with $100 initial principal and 1% interest per month would have a balance of $101 at the end of the first month, $102.01 at the end of the second month, and so on.
Continuous	In mathematics, a continuous function is a function for which, intuitively, small changes in the input result in small changes in the output. Otherwise, a function is said to be discontinuous. A continuous function with a continuous inverse function is called bicontinuous.

Chapter 3. How to Calculate Present Values

Chapter 4. Valuing Bonds

Bond valuation	Bond valuation is the process of determining the fair price of a bond.
	As with any security or capital investment, the fair value of a bond is the present value of the stream of cash flows it is expected to generate. Hence, the value of a bond is determined by discounting the bond''s expected cash flows to the present using the appropriate discount rate.
Debt	Debt is that which is owed; usually referencing assets owed, but the term can also cover moral obligations and other interactions not requiring money. In the case of assets, Debt is a means of using future purchasing power in the present before a summation has been earned. Some companies and corporations use Debt as a part of their overall corporate finance strategy.
Dot-com bubble	The "dot-com bubble" (or) was a speculative bubble covering roughly 1998-2001 (with a climax on March 10, 2000 with the NASDAQ peaking at 5132.52) during which stock markets in Western nations saw their equity value rise rapidly from growth in the more recent Internet sector and related fields. While the latter part was a boom and bust cycle, the Internet boom sometimes is meant to refer to the steady commercial growth of the Internet with the advent of the world wide web as exemplified by the first release of the Mosaic web browser in 1993 and continuing through the 1990s.
	The period was marked by the founding (and, in many cases, spectacular failure) of a group of new Internet-based companies commonly referred to as dot-coms.
Treasury bonds	A United States Treasury security is a government debt issued by the United States Department of the Treasury through the Bureau of the Public Debt. Treasury securities are the debt financing instruments of the United States Federal government, and they are often referred to simply as Treasuries. There are four types of marketable treasury securities: Treasury bills, Treasury notes, treasury Bonds, and Treasury Inflation Protected Securities (TIPS).
Yield to maturity	The yield to maturity or redemption yield of a bond or other fixed-interest security, such as gilts, is the internal rate of return (IRR, overall interest rate) earned by an investor who buys the bond today at the market price, assuming that the bond will be held until maturity, and that all coupon and principal payments will be made on schedule. yield to maturity is actually an estimation of future return, as the rate at which coupon payments can be reinvested when received is unknown. It enables investors to compare the merits of different financial instruments.
Capital market	A Capital market is a market for securities (both debt and equity), where business enterprises (companies) and governments can raise long-term funds. It is defined as a market in which money is lent for periods longer than a year, as the raising of short-term funds takes place on other markets (e.g., the money market). The Capital market includes the stock market (equity securities) and the bond market (debt).
Present value	Present value is the value on a given date of a future payment or series of future payments, discounted to reflect the time value of money and other factors such as investment risk. Present value calculations are widely used in business and economics to provide a means to compare cash flows at different times on a meaningful "like to like" basis.
	If offered a choice between $100 today or $100 in one year, a rational person will choose $100 today.
Bid price	A Bid price is the highest price that a buyer (i.e., bidder) is willing to pay for a good. It is usually referred to simply as the "bid."
	In bid and ask, the Bid price stands in contrast to the ask price or "offer", and the difference between the two is called the bid/ask spread.
	An unsolicited bid or offer is when a person or company receives a bid even though they are not looking to sell.

Chapter 4. Valuing Bonds

Chapter 4. Valuing Bonds

Discounted cash flow	In finance, the Discounted cash flow approach describes a method of valuing a project, company, that reflects the risk of the cashflows.
Duration	In finance, the Duration of a financial asset measures the sensitivity of the asset"s price to interest rate movements. There are various definitions of Duration and derived quantities, discussed below. If not otherwise specified, "Duration" generally means the Macaulay Duration, as defined below.
Net present value	Net present value or net present worth (NPW) is defined as the total present value (PV) of a time series of cash flows. It is a standard method for using the time value of money to appraise long-term projects. Used for capital budgeting, and widely throughout economics, it measures the excess or shortfall of cash flows, in present value terms, once financing charges are met.
Variance	In probability theory and statistics, the Variance of a random variable or distribution is the expected square deviation of that variable from its expected value or mean). For example, a perfect die, when thrown, has expected value 7/2, expected deviation 3/2 (the mean of the equally likely absolute deviations 1/2, 3/2, 5/2), but expected square deviation 35/12 ≈ 2.9 (the mean of the equally likely squared deviations 1/4, 9/4, and 25/4). As another example, the two roots of the quadratic $ax^2 + bx + c$ have mean the root of its derivative $2ax + b$, namely $x = -b/2a$, and Variance its discriminant $b^2 - 4ac$ divided by $4a^2$, this being the square deviation of each root from the mean.
Interest	In the Renaissance era, greater mobility of people facilitated an increase in commerce and the appearance of appropriate conditions for entrepreneurs to start new, lucrative businesses. Given that borrowed money was no longer strictly for consumption but for production as well, Interest was no longer viewed in the same manner. The School of Salamanca elaborated on various reasons that justified the charging of Interest: the person who received a loan benefited, and one could consider Interest as a premium paid for the risk taken by the loaning party.
Interest rates	An interest rate is the price a borrower pays for the use of money they do not own, for instance a small company might borrow from a bank to kick start their business, and the return a lender receives for deferring the use of funds, by lending it to the borrower. Interest rates are normally expressed as a percentage rate over the period of one year. Interest rates targets are also a vital tool of monetary policy and are used to control variables like investment, inflation, and unemployment.
Portfolio theory	Modern portfolio theory (MPT) is a theory of investment which attempts to explain how investors can maximize return and minimize risk. Although MPT is widely used in practice in the financial industry and several of its creators won a Nobel prize for the theory, in recent years the basic assumptions of MPT have been widely challenged by fields such as behavioral economics, and many companies using variants of MPT have gone bankrupt in various financial crises. MPT is a mathematical formulation of the concept of diversification in investing, with the aim of selecting a collection of investment assets that has collectively lower risk than any individual asset.
Interest rate risk	Interest rate risk is the risk (variability in value) borne by an interest-bearing asset, such as a loan or a bond, due to variability of interest rates. In general, as rates rise, the price of a fixed rate bond will fall, and vice versa. Interest rate risk is commonly measured by the bond"s duration.

Chapter 4. Valuing Bonds

Yield curve

In finance, the yield curve is the relation between the interest rate (or cost of borrowing) and the time to maturity of the debt for a given borrower in a given currency. For example, the U.S. dollar interest rates paid on U.S. Treasury securities for various maturities are closely watched by many traders, and are commonly plotted on a graph such as the one on the right which is informally called "the yield curve." More formal mathematical descriptions of this relation are often called the term structure of interest rates.

The yield of a debt instrument is the overall rate of return available on the investment.

Securities

A security is a fungible, negotiable instrument representing financial value. Securities are broadly categorized into debt Securities (such as banknotes, bonds and debentures); equity Securities, e.g., common stocks; and derivative contracts, such as forwards, futures, options and swaps. The company or other entity issuing the security is called the issuer.

Consumer

consumer is a broad label that refers to any individuals or households that use goods and services generated within the economy. The concept of a consumer is used in different contexts, so that the usage and significance of the term may vary.

Typically when business people and economists talk of consumers they are talking about person as consumer, an aggregated commodity item with little individuality other than that expressed in the buy/not-buy decision.

Consumer Price Index

A Consumer price index is a measure estimating the average price of consumer goods and services purchased by households. A Consumer price index measures a price change for a constant market basket of goods and services from one period to the next within the same area (city, region, or nation). It is a price index determined by measuring the price of a standard group of goods meant to represent the typical market basket of a typical urban consumer.

Depression

In economics, a depression is a sustained, long-term downturn in economic activity in one or more economies. It is a more severe downturn than a recession, which is seen as part of a normal business cycle.

Considered a rare and extreme form of recession, a depression is characterized by its length, and by abnormal increases in unemployment, falls in the availability of credit, shrinking output and investment, numerous bankruptcies, reduced amounts of trade and commerce, as well as highly volatile relative currency value fluctuations, mostly devaluations.

Great Depression

The Great Depression was a severe worldwide economic depression in the decade preceding World War II. The timing of the Great Depression varied across nations, but in most countries it started in about 1929 and lasted until the late 1930s or early 1940s. It was the longest, most widespread, and deepest depression of the 20th century, and is used in the 21st century as an example of how far the world"s economy can decline. The depression originated in the United States, triggered by the stock market crash of October 29, 1929 (known as Black Tuesday), but quickly spread to almost every country in the world.

Inflation

In economics, Inflation is a rise in the general level of prices of goods and services in an economy over a period of time. When the price level rises, each unit of currency buys fewer goods and services; consequently, Inflation is also an erosion in the purchasing power of money - a loss of real value in the internal medium of exchange and unit of account in the economy. A chief measure of price Inflation is the Inflation rate, the annualized percentage change in a general price index (normally the Consumer Price Index) over time.

Chapter 4. Valuing Bonds

Bank	A Bank is a financial institution licensed by a government. Its primary activities include borrowing and lending money. Many other financial activities were allowed over time.
Loan	A Loan is a type of debt. Like all debt instruments, a Loan entails the redistribution of financial assets over time, between the lender and the borrower.
	In a Loan, the borrower initially receives or borrows an amount of money, called the principal, from the lender, and is obligated to pay back or repay an equal amount of money to the lender at a later time.
Nominal interest rate	In finance and economics Nominal interest rate or nominal rate of interest refers to the rate of interest before adjustment for inflation (in contrast with the real interest rate); or, for interest rates "as stated" without adjustment for the full effect of compounding (also referred to as the nominal annual rate). An interest rate is called nominal if the frequency of compounding (e.g. a month) is not identical to the basic time unit (normally a year).
	The real interest rate includes compensation for the lender"s lost value due to inflation, whereas the Nominal interest rate excludes inflation.
Real Interest rate	The "Real interest rate" is approximately the nominal interest rate minus the inflation rate . Since the inflation rate over the course of a loan is not known initially, volatility in inflation represents a risk to both the lender and the borrower.
	In economics and finance, an individual who lends money for repayment at a later point in time expects to be compensated for the time value of money, or not having the use of that money while it is lent.

Chapter 5. The Value of Common Stocks

Equity	Equity, in finance and accounting, refers to the residual claim or interest of the most junior class of investors in an asset, after all liabilities are paid. If valuations placed on assets do not exceed liabilities, negative Equity exists. In an accounting context, Shareholders" Equity (or stockholders" Equity, shareholders" funds, shareholders" capital or similar terms) represents the remaining interest in assets of a company, spread among individual shareholders of common or preferred stock.
Common stock	Common stock is a form of corporate equity ownership, a type of security. It is called "common" to distinguish it from preferred stock. In the event of bankruptcy, Common stock investors receive their funds after preferred stock holders, bondholders, creditors, etc.
Valuation	In finance, valuation is the process of estimating the potential market value of a financial asset or liability. valuations can be done on assets (for example, investments in marketable securities such as stocks, options, business enterprises, or intangible assets such as patents and trademarks) or on liabilities (e.g., Bonds issued by a company). valuations are required in many contexts including investment analysis, capital budgeting, merger and acquisition transactions, financial reporting, taxable events to determine the proper tax liability, and in litigation. valuation of financial assets is done using one or more of these types of models: · Discounted Cash Flows determine the value by estimating the expected future earnings from owning the asset discounted to their present value. · Relative value models determine the value based on the market prices of similar assets. · Option pricing models are used for certain types of financial assets (e.g., warrants, put options, call options, employee stock options, investments with embedded options such as a callable bond) and are a complex present value model.
Dividend	Dividends are payments made by a corporation to its shareholder members. It is the portion of corporate profits paid out to stockholders. When a corporation earns a profit or surplus, that money can be put to two uses: it can either be re-invested in the business (called retained earnings), or it can be paid to the shareholders as a Dividend.
New York Stock Exchange	The New York Stock Exchange is a stock exchange located at 11 Wall Street in lower Manhattan, New York City, New York, USA. It is the largest stock exchange in the world by United States dollar value of its listed companies" securities. As of October 2008, the combined capitalization of all domestic New York Stock Exchange listed companies was US$10.1 trillion. The New York Stock Exchange is operated by New York Stock Exchange Euronext, which was formed by the New York Stock Exchange "s 2007 merger with the fully-electronic stock exchange Euronext.
Primary market	The Primary market is that part of the capital markets that deals with the issuance of new securities. Companies, governments or public sector institutions can obtain funding through the sale of a new stock or bond issue. This is typically done through a syndicate of securities dealers.
Correlation swap	A Correlation swap is an over-the-counter financial derivative that allows one to speculate on or hedge risks associated with the observed average correlation, of a collection of underlying products, where each product has periodically observable prices, as with a commodity, exchange rate, interest rate, while the floating leg pays the annualized realized correlation $\rho_{realized}$. The contract value at expiration from the pay-fixed perspective is therefore $N_{corr}(\rho_{realized} - \rho_{strike})$

Chapter 5. The Value of Common Stocks

Given a set of nonnegative weights w_i on n securities, with observed pairwise correlations measured to be $\rho_{i,j}$ the weighted average correlation is defined as

$$\rho_{\text{realized}} = \frac{\sum_{i,j} w_i w_j \rho_{i,j}}{\sum_{i,j} w_i w_j}$$

No industry-standard models yet exist that have stochastic correlation and are arbitrage-free.

Stock exchange	A Stock exchange is a corporation or mutual organization which provides "trading" facilities for stock brokers and traders, to trade stocks and other securities. Stock exchanges also provide facilities for the issue and redemption of securities as well as other financial instruments and capital events including the payment of income and dividends. The securities traded on a Stock exchange include: shares issued by companies, unit trusts, derivatives, pooled investment products and bonds.
Capital market	A Capital market is a market for securities (both debt and equity), where business enterprises (companies) and governments can raise long-term funds. It is defined as a market in which money is lent for periods longer than a year, as the raising of short-term funds takes place on other markets (e.g., the money market). The Capital market includes the stock market (equity securities) and the bond market (debt).
Efficient-market hypothesis	In finance, the Efficient-market hypothesis (EMH) asserts that financial markets are "informationally efficient", stocks, bonds, or property) already reflect all known information, and instantly change to reflect new information. Therefore, according to theory, it is impossible to consistently outperform the market by using any information that the market already knows, except through luck. Information or news in the EMH is defined as anything that may affect prices that is unknowable in the present and thus appears randomly in the future.
Stock split	A Stock split or stock divide increases or decreases the number of shares in a public company. The price is adjusted such that the market capitalization of the company remains the same after the split, so that dilution does not occur. Options and warrants are included.
Dalal Street	Dalal Street (Marathi: à¤¦à¤²à¤¾à¤² - DalÄ l means a broker) in downtown Mumbai, India is the address of the Bombay Stock Exchange (in the Phiroze Jeejeebhoy Towers) and several related financial firms and institutions.It is the busiest street in the city. When Bombay Stock Exchange was moved to this new location at the intersection of Bombay SamÄ chÄ r Marg and Hammam Street, the street next to the building was renamed as Dalal Street. Similar to Wall Street in New York City, it is often used as a metonym for the entire Indian financial establishment.
Exchange-traded fund	An Exchange-traded fund (or ETF) is an investment vehicle traded on stock exchanges, much like stocks. An ETF holds assets such as stocks or bonds and trades at approximately the same price as the net asset value of its underlying assets over the course of the trading day. Most ETFs track an index, such as the S'P 500 or MSCI EAFE. ETFs may be attractive as investments because of their low costs, tax efficiency, and stock-like features.
Mutual fund	A Mutual fund is a professionally managed type of collective investment scheme that pools money from many investors and invests it in stocks, bonds, short-term money market instruments, and/or other securities. The Mutual fund will have a fund manager that trades the pooled money on a regular basis. The net proceeds or losses are then typically distributed to the investors annually.

Chapter 5. The Value of Common Stocks

Chapter 5. The Value of Common Stocks

Dot-com bubble	The "dot-com bubble" (or) was a speculative bubble covering roughly 1998-2001 (with a climax on March 10, 2000 with the NASDAQ peaking at 5132.52) during which stock markets in Western nations saw their equity value rise rapidly from growth in the more recent Internet sector and related fields. While the latter part was a boom and bust cycle, the Internet boom sometimes is meant to refer to the steady commercial growth of the Internet with the advent of the world wide web as exemplified by the first release of the Mosaic web browser in 1993 and continuing through the 1990s. The period was marked by the founding (and, in many cases, spectacular failure) of a group of new Internet-based companies commonly referred to as dot-coms.
Return	Returns .
Cost	In business, retail, and accounting, a cost is the value of money that has been used up to produce something, and hence is not available for use anymore. In economics, a cost is an alternative that is given up as a result of a decision. In business, the cost may be one of acquisition, in which case the amount of money expended to acquire it is counted as cost.
Cost of equity	In finance, the cost of equity is the minimum rate of return a firm must offer shareholders to compensate for waiting for their returns, and for bearing some risk. The cost of equity capital for a particular company is the rate of return on investment that is required by the company"s ordinary shareholders. The return consists both of dividend and capital gains, e.g. increases in the share price.
Discounted cash flow	In finance, the Discounted cash flow approach describes a method of valuing a project, company, that reflects the risk of the cashflows.
Market capitalization	Market capitalization/capitalisation (often market cap) is a measurement of the size of a business enterprise (corporation) equal to the share price times the number of shares outstanding of a public company. As owning stock represents ownership of the company, including all its equity, capitalization could represent the public opinion of a company"s net worth and is a determining factor in stock valuation. Likewise, the capitalization of stock markets or economic regions may be compared to other economic indicators.
Macro derivative	A macro derivative or an economic derivative is a derivative that is based on a macroeconomic figure, such as consumer confidence, jobless claims, in 2002 Goldman Sachs and Deutsche Bank announced to offer their clients auctions for derivatives based on macroeconomic key figures. In 2005 Deutsche Bank left the joint project.
Business valuation	Business valuation is a process and a set of procedures used to estimate the economic value of an owner"s interest in a business. Valuation is used by financial market participants to determine the price they are willing to pay or receive to consummate a sale of a business. In addition to estimating the selling price of a business, the same valuation tools are often used by business appraisers to resolve disputes related to estate and gift taxation, divorce litigation, allocate business purchase price among business assets, establish a formula for estimating the value of partners" ownership interest for buy-sell agreements, and many other business and legal purposes.
Capitalization rate	Capitalization rate (or "cap rate") is the ratio between the net operating income produced by an asset and its capital cost (the original price paid to buy the asset) or alternatively its current market value. The rate is calculated in a simple fashion as follows: $$\text{Capitalization Rate} = \frac{\text{annual net operating income}}{\text{cost (or value)}}$$

Chapter 5. The Value of Common Stocks

For example, if a building is purchased for $1,000,000 sale price and it produces $100,000 in positive net operating income during one year, then:

- $100,000 / $1,000,000 = 0.10 = 10%

The asset"s Capitalization rate is ten percent.

If the owner bought the building twenty years ago for $200,000, his cap rate is

- $100,000 / $200,000 = 0.50 = 50%.

Or is it? The investor has to take into account the opportunity cost of keeping his money tied up in this investment. By keeping this building, he is losing the opportunity of investing $1,000,000 (by selling the building at its market value and investing the proceeds).

Dividend payout ratio

Dividend payout ratio is the fraction of net income a firm pays to its stockholders in dividends:

$$\text{Dividend payout ratio} = \frac{\text{Dividends}}{\text{Net Income for the same period}}$$

The part of the earnings not paid to investors is left for investment to provide for future earnings growth. Investors seeking high current income and limited capital growth prefer companies with high Dividend payout ratio. However investors seeking capital growth may prefer lower payout ratio because capital gains are taxed at a lower rate.

Call option

A Call option is a financial contract between two parties, the buyer and the seller of this type of option. It is the option to buy shares of stock at a specified time in the future. Often it is simply labeled a "call".

Dividend yield

The Dividend yield or the dividend-price ratio on a company stock is the company"s annual dividend payments divided by its market cap

Performance measurement

Performance measurement is the process whereby an organization establishes the parameters within which programs, investments, and acquisitions are reaching the desired results. Performance Reference Model of the Federal Enterprise Architecture, 2005.

This process of measuring performance often requires the use of statistical evidence to determine progress toward specific defined organizational objectives.

There are many types of measurements.

Incentive

In economics and sociology, an incentive is any factor (financial or non-financial) that enables or motivates a particular course of action, the study of incentive structures is central to the study of all economic activity (both in terms of individual decision-making and in terms of co-operation and competition within a larger institutional structure).

Payout ratio

Dividend payout ratio is the fraction of net income a firm pays to its stockholders in dividends:

$$\text{Dividend payout ratio} = \frac{\text{Dividends}}{\text{Net Income for the same period}}$$

The part of the earnings not paid to investors is left for investment to provide for future earnings growth. Investors seeking high current income and limited capital growth prefer companies with high Dividend payout ratio. However investors seeking capital growth may prefer lower payout ratio because capital gains are taxed at a lower rate.

Chapter 5. The Value of Common Stocks

Chapter 5. The Value of Common Stocks

Return on equity	Return on equity (Return on equity, Return on average common equity, return on net worth, Return on ordinary shareholders" funds) (requity) measures the rate of return on the ownership interest (shareholders" equity) of the common stock owners. It measures a firm"s efficiency at generating profits from every unit of shareholders" equity (also known as net assets or assets minus liabilities). Return on equity shows how well a company uses investment funds to generate earnings growth.
Functional classification	The functional classification of a road is the class, of roads that the road belongs to. There are three main functional classes as defined by the United States Federal Highway Administration: arterial, collector, and local. Arterial roads generally provide the fastest method of travel and typically have low accessibility from neighboring roads.
Santa Fe	Santa Fe or Santa Fé may be: Argentina: · Santa Fe, Argentina · Santa Fe Province Brazil: · Santa Fé, Paraná · Santa Fé de Goiás · Santa Fé de Minas (Minas Gerais) · Santa Fé do Sul (São Paulo) · Santa Fé do Araguaia (Tocantins) · Bonito de Santa Fé (Paraíba) Colombia: · Santa Fe de Bogotá, also Santafé de Bogotá, former name of Bogotá, the nation"s capital · Santa Fe de Ralito · Santa Fe C.D. Cuba: · Santa Fe, Isle of Youth, on the Isle of Youth · Santa Fe, Havana Ecuador: · Santa Fe Island, one of the Galápagos Islands Honduras: · Santa Fe, Colón · Santa Fé, Ocotepeque Mexico:

Chapter 5. The Value of Common Stocks

- Santa Fe, Baja California Sur
- Santa Fe, Chihuahua
- Santa Fe, Coahuila
- Santa Fe, Guanajuato
- Santa Fe, Jalisco
- Santa Fe (Mexico City), within Mexico City
- Santa Fe, Michoacán
- Santa Fe, Nayarit
- Santa Fe, Nuevo León
- Santa Fe, Sinaloa
- Santa Fe, Veracruz

Panama:

- Santa Fé, Veraguas
- Santa Fé, Darién

Philippines:

- Santa Fe, Cebu
- Santa Fe, Leyte
- Santa Fe, Nueva Vizcaya
- Santa Fe, Romblon

Spain:

- Santa Fe, Granada
- Santa Fe, Catalonia
- Santa Fe del Penedès (Catalonia)
- Santa Fe de Mondújar (Almería)

United States:

- Santa Fe, Florida
- Santa Fe, Indiana
- Santa Fe, Missouri
- Santa Fe, New Mexico, state capital of New Mexico
- Santa Fe, Ohio
- Santa Fe, Tennessee
- Santa Fe, Texas
- Santa Fe Springs, California
- Santa Fe County, New Mexico
- Rancho Santa Fe, California

Venezuela:

- Santa Fe, Falcón
- Santa Fe, Sucre

Chapter 5. The Value of Common Stocks

Chapter 5. The Value of Common Stocks

- Santa Fe de Nuevo México, a province of New Spain that existed from the late 16th century up through the early 19th century
- Santa Fe Trail, a historic 19th century transportation route across southwestern North America
- New Santa Fe Trail, an auto trail in the United States connecting Kansas City, Missouri with Los Angeles, California
- Lake Santa Fe, lake in northeastern Alachua County, Florida, USA
- Santa Fe River (Florida), a tributary of the Suwannee River, USA
- Santa Fe River (New Mexico), USA
- Santa Fe National Forest, a protected national forest in northern New Mexico in the southwestern United States.

- Santa Fe (group), a Cuban band
- Santa Fe (nude photo book), a title of Japanese actress Rie Miyazawa"s nude photo book
- Santa Fe Trail , a 1940 Western
- Santa Fe Passage, a 1955 American western movie
- Santa Fe (1951 film) a 1951 Western starring Randolph Scott
- Santa Fe (Jon Bon Jovi song), a song from the Jon Bon Jovi"s album Blaze of Glory

- Atchison, Topeka and Santa Fe Railway, often abbreviated as the "Santa Fe"
- Santa Fe de Luxe, the first extra-fare named passenger train on the Atchison, Topeka and Santa Fe Railway.

- Santa Fe Depot, original name of Union Station (San Diego), a train and bus terminus
- Hyundai Santa Fe, a sport utility vehicle
- USS Santa Fe, two US Navy ships named after Santa Fe, New Mexico
- ARA Santa Fe, multiple vessels in the Argentine navy

- Texas Santa Fe Expedition, an expedition to claim parts of northern New Mexico for Texas in 1841
- Santa Fe Natural Tobacco Company, a tobacco manufacturer
- Disney"s Hotel Santa Fe, a hotel at Disneyland Resort Paris
- Santa Fe College, in Gainesville, Florida, USA
- Santa Fe Community College, in Santa Fe, New Mexico, USA
- Santa Fe Institute - research of complex systems
- Santa Fé de Toloca, Spanish mission established within sight of the Santa Fe River in Florida, between 1606 and 1616 .

Comprehensive income	Comprehensive income (or earnings) is a specific term used in companies" financial reporting from the company-whole point of view. Because that use excludes the effects of changing ownership interest, an economic measure of Comprehensive income is necessary for financial analysis from the shareholders" point of view
	Comprehensive income is defined by the Financial Accounting Standards Board, or FASB, as "the change in equity [net assets] of a business enterprise during a period from transactions and other events and circumstances from nonowner sources. It includes all changes in equity during a period except those resulting from investments by owners and distributions to owners."

Chapter 5. The Value of Common Stocks

	Comprehensive income is the sum of net income and other items that must bypass the income statement because they have not been realized, including items like an unrealized holding gain or loss from available for sale securities and foreign currency translation gains or losses.
Earnings per share	Earnings per share are the earnings returned on the initial investment amount.
	In the US, the Financial Accounting Standards Board (FASB) requires companies" income statements to report Earnings per share for each of the major categories of the income statement: continuing operations, discontinued operations, extraordinary items, and net income.
	The Earnings per share formula does not include preferred dividends for categories outside of continued operations and net income.
Growth stock	In finance, Growth stocks are stocks belonging to companies that have shown high growth (e.g. in earnings) in the past and, it is hoped, will continue to grow, leading to good investor returns.
	Analysts compute ROE by taking the company"s net income and dividing it by the company"s equity. To be classified as a Growth stock, analysts expect to see at least 15 percent return on equity.
Net present value	Net present value or net present worth (NPW) is defined as the total present value (PV) of a time series of cash flows. It is a standard method for using the time value of money to appraise long-term projects. Used for capital budgeting, and widely throughout economics, it measures the excess or shortfall of cash flows, in present value terms, once financing charges are met.
Free cash flow	In corporate finance, Free cash flow is cash flow available for distribution among all the securities holders of an organization. They include equity holders, debt holders, preferred stock holders, convertible security holders, and so on.
	Note that the first three lines above are calculated for you on the standard Statement of Cash Flows.
Adjusted present value	Adjusted present value is a business valuation method. Adjusted present value is the net present value of a project if financed solely by ownership equity plus the present value of all the benefits of financing. It was first studied by Stewart Myers, a professor at the MIT Sloan School of Management and later theorized by Lorenzo Peccati, professor at the Bocconi University, in 1973.
	The method is to calculate the NPV of the project as if it is all-equity financed (so called base case).
Bond valuation	Bond valuation is the process of determining the fair price of a bond.
	As with any security or capital investment, the fair value of a bond is the present value of the stream of cash flows it is expected to generate. Hence, the value of a bond is determined by discounting the bond"s expected cash flows to the present using the appropriate discount rate.

Chapter 6. Why Net Present Value Leads to Better Investment Decisions than Other Criteria

Monte Carlo methods	Monte Carlo methods are a class of computational algorithms that rely on repeated random sampling to compute their results. Monte Carlo methods are often used when simulating physical and mathematical systems. Because of their reliance on repeated computation of random or pseudo-random numbers, Monte Carlo methods are most suited to calculation by a computer.
Investment	Investment or investing is a term with several closely-related meanings in business management, finance and economics, related to saving or deferring consumption. Investing is the active redirection of resources: from being consumed today, to creating benefits in the future; the use of assets to earn income or profit. An Investment is a choice by an individual or an organization such as a pension fund, after at least some careful analysis or thought, to place or lend money in a vehicle (e.g. property, stock securities, bonds) that has sufficiently low risk and provides the possibility of generating returns over a period of time.
Investment decisions	Investment decisions are made by investors and investment managers. Investors commonly perform investment analysis by making use of fundamental analysis, technical analysis and gut feel. Investment decisions are often supported by decision tools.
Capital budgeting	Capital budgeting (or investment appraisal) is the planning process used to determine whether a firm"s long term investments such as new machinery, replacement machinery, new plants, new products, and research development projects are worth pursuing. It is budget for major capital, or investment, expenditures. Many formal methods are used in Capital budgeting, including the techniques such as · Accounting rate of return · Net present value · Profitability index · Internal rate of return · Modified Internal Rate of Return · Equivalent annuity These methods use the incremental cash flows from each potential investment, or project Techniques based on accounting earnings and accounting rules are sometimes used - though economists consider this to be improper - such as the accounting rate of return, and "return on investment." Simplified and hybrid methods are used as well, such as payback period and discounted payback period. Each potential project"s value should be estimated using a discounted cash flow (DCF) valuation, to find its net present value (NPV).
Cash flow	Cash flow refers to the movement of cash into or out of a business, a project, finite period of time. Measurement of Cash flow can be used · to determine a project"s rate of return or value. The time of Cash flows into and out of projects are used as inputs in financial models such as internal rate of return, and net present value. · to determine problems with a business"s liquidity.
Discount rate	The Discount rate is an interest rate a central bank charges depository institutions that borrow reserves from it. The term Discount rate has two meanings:

Chapter 6. Why Net Present Value Leads to Better Investment Decisions than Other Criteria

Chapter 6. Why Net Present Value Leads to Better Investment Decisions than Other Criteria

· the same as interest rate; the term "discount" does not refer to the meaning of the word, but to the purpose of using the quantity, such as computations of present value, e.g. net present value or discounted cash flow

· the annual effective Discount rate, which is the annual interest divided by the capital including that interest; this rate is lower than the interest rate; it corresponds to using the value after a year as the nominal value, and seeing the initial value as the nominal value minus a discount; it is used for Treasury Bills and similar financial instruments

The annual effective Discount rate is the annual interest divided by the capital including that interest, which is the interest rate divided by 100% plus the interest rate. It is the annual discount factor to be applied to the future cash flow, to find the discount, subtracted from a future value to find the value one year earlier.

For example, suppose there is a government bond that sells for $95 and pays $100 in a year"s time.

Discounted cash flow	In finance, the Discounted cash flow approach describes a method of valuing a project, company, that reflects the risk of the cashflows.
Opportunity cost	Opportunity cost or economic opportunity loss is the value of the next best alternative forgone as the result of making a decision. Opportunity cost analysis is an important part of a company"s decision-making processes but is not treated as an actual cost in any financial statement. The next best thing that a person can engage in is referred to as the Opportunity cost of doing the best thing and ignoring the next best thing to be done.
Opportunity cost of capital	The opportunity cost of capital is the expected return forgone by bypassing of other potential investment activities for a given capital. It is a rate of return that investors could earn in financial markets. .
Adjustment	Adjustment means regulating, adapting or settling in a variety of contexts:
	Adjustment has several meanings; many relate to insurance, contracts, or the resolution of disputes.
	In Engineering, Mathematics and Geodesy, Adjustment means the optimal parameter estimation of a mathematical model so as to best fit a data set. The most important method is the least squares Adjustment, found by Carl Friedrich Gauss.
Financial statements	financial statements (or financial reports) are formal records of the financial activities of a business, person, including United Kingdom company law, financial statements are often referred to as accounts, although the term financial statements is also used, particularly by accountants.
	financial statements provide an overview of a business or person"s financial condition in both short and long term.
Forecasting	forecasting is the process of estimation in unknown situations. Prediction is a similar, but more general term. Both can refer to estimation of time series, cross-sectional or longitudinal data.
Net present value	Net present value or net present worth (NPW) is defined as the total present value (PV) of a time series of cash flows. It is a standard method for using the time value of money to appraise long-term projects. Used for capital budgeting, and widely throughout economics, it measures the excess or shortfall of cash flows, in present value terms, once financing charges are met.
Rate of return	Yield is the compound Rate of return that includes the effect of reinvesting interest or dividends.
	To the right is an example of a stock investment of one share purchased at the beginning of the year for $100.

Chapter 6. Why Net Present Value Leads to Better Investment Decisions than Other Criteria

Chapter 6. Why Net Present Value Leads to Better Investment Decisions than Other Criteria

· The quarterly dividend is reinvested at the quarter-end stock price.
· The number of shares purchased each quarter = ($ Dividend)/($ Stock Price).
· The final investment value of $103.02 is a 3.02% Yield on the initial investment of $100. This is the compound yield, and this return can be considered to be the return on the investment of $100.
To calculate the Rate of return, the investor includes the reinvested dividends in the total investment. The investor received a total of $4.06 in dividends over the year, all of which were reinvested, so the investment amount increased by $4.06.

· Total Investment = Cost Basis = $100 + $4.06 = $104.06.
· Capital gain/loss = $103.02 - $104.06 = -$1.04 (a capital loss)
· ($4.06 dividends - $1.04 capital loss) / $104.06 total investment = 2.9% ROI

The disadvantage of this ROI calculation is that it does not take into account the fact that not all the money was invested during the entire year (the dividend reinvestments occurred throughout the year).

Internality	An internality is a term used in behavioral economics to describe those types of behaviors that impose costs on a person in the long-run that are not taken into account when making decisions in the present. Classical Economics discourages government from creating legislation that targets internalities, because it is assumed that the consumer takes these personal costs into account when paying for the good that causes the internality. For example, cigarettes should be taxed because of the negative consumption externalities that they impose, such as second-hand smoke, not because the smoker harms him or herself by smoking.
Internal rate of return	The internal rate of return (IRR) is a rate of return used in capital budgeting to measure and compare the profitability of investments. It is also called the discounted cash flow rate of return (DCFROR) or simply the rate of return (ROR). In the context of savings and loans the IRR is also called the effective interest rate.
Payback period	payback period in business and economics refers to the period of time required for the return on an investment to "repay" the sum of the original investment. For example, a $1000 investment which returned $500 per year would have a two year payback period. It intuitively measures how long something takes to "pay for itself." Shorter payback periods are obviously preferable to longer payback periods (all else being equal).
Profitability index	profitability index identifies the relationship of investment to payoff of a proposed project. The ratio is calculated as follows: $$\text{Profitability index} = \frac{\text{PV of future cash flows}}{\text{PV of initial investment}}$$ profitability index is also known as Profit Investment Ratio, abbreviated to P.I. and Value Investment Ratio (V.I.R).. profitability index is a good tool for ranking projects because it allows you to clearly identify the amount of value created per unit of investment, thus if you are capital constrained you wish to invest in those projects which create value most efficiently first. Nota Bene; Statements below this paragraph assume the cash flow calculated does not include the investment made in the project.

Chapter 6. Why Net Present Value Leads to Better Investment Decisions than Other Criteria

Chapter 6. Why Net Present Value Leads to Better Investment Decisions than Other Criteria

Debt	Debt is that which is owed; usually referencing assets owed, but the term can also cover moral obligations and other interactions not requiring money. In the case of assets, Debt is a means of using future purchasing power in the present before a summation has been earned. Some companies and corporations use Debt as a part of their overall corporate finance strategy.
Capital structure	In finance, Capital structure refers to the way a corporation finances its assets through some combination of equity, debt, a firm that sells $20 billion in equity and $80 billion in debt is said to be 20% equity-financed and 80% debt-financed.
Rule of signs	In mathematics, Descartes" Rule of signs, first described by René Descartes in his work La Géométrie, is a technique for determining the number of positive or negative roots of a polynomial.
	The rule gives us an upper bound number of positive or negative roots of a polynomial. It is not a deterministic rule, ie it does not tell the exact number of positive or negative roots.
Mutually exclusive	In layman"s terms, two events are mutually exclusive if they cannot occur at the same time (i.e., they have no common outcomes).
	In logic, two mutually exclusive propositions are propositions that logically cannot both be true. Another term f is "disjunct." To say that more than two propositions are mutually exclusive may, depending on context mean that no two of them can both be true, or only that they cannot all be true.
Yield curve	In finance, the yield curve is the relation between the interest rate (or cost of borrowing) and the time to maturity of the debt for a given borrower in a given currency. For example, the U.S. dollar interest rates paid on U.S. Treasury securities for various maturities are closely watched by many traders, and are commonly plotted on a graph such as the one on the right which is informally called "the yield curve." More formal mathematical descriptions of this relation are often called the term structure of interest rates.
	The yield of a debt instrument is the overall rate of return available on the investment.
Interest	In the Renaissance era, greater mobility of people facilitated an increase in commerce and the appearance of appropriate conditions for entrepreneurs to start new, lucrative businesses. Given that borrowed money was no longer strictly for consumption but for production as well, Interest was no longer viewed in the same manner. The School of Salamanca elaborated on various reasons that justified the charging of Interest: the person who received a loan benefited, and one could consider Interest as a premium paid for the risk taken by the loaning party.
Interest rates	An interest rate is the price a borrower pays for the use of money they do not own, for instance a small company might borrow from a bank to kick start their business, and the return a lender receives for deferring the use of funds, by lending it to the borrower. Interest rates are normally expressed as a percentage rate over the period of one year.
	Interest rates targets are also a vital tool of monetary policy and are used to control variables like investment, inflation, and unemployment.
Rationing	Rationing is the controlled distribution of resources and scarce goods or services. Rationing controls the size of the ration, one"s allotted portion of the resources being distributed on a particular day or at a particular time.
	In economics, it is often common to use the word "Rationing" to refer to one of the roles that prices play in markets, while Rationing (as the word is usually used) is called "non-price Rationing".

Chapter 6. Why Net Present Value Leads to Better Investment Decisions than Other Criteria

Linear programming	In mathematics, linear programming is a technique for optimization of a linear objective function, subject to linear equality and linear inequality constraints. Informally, linear programming determines the way to achieve the best outcome (such as maximum profit or lowest cost) in a given mathematical model and given some list of requirements represented as linear equations.

More formally, given a polytope (for example, a polygon or a polyhedron), and a real-valued affine function

$$f(x_1, x_2, \ldots, x_n) = c_1 x_1 + c_2 x_2 + \cdots + c_n x_n + d$$

defined on this polytope, a linear programming method will find a point in the polytope where this function has the smallest (or largest) value.

Chapter 7. Making Investment Decisions with the Net Present Value Rule

Net present value	Net present value or net present worth (NPW) is defined as the total present value (PV) of a time series of cash flows. It is a standard method for using the time value of money to appraise long-term projects. Used for capital budgeting, and widely throughout economics, it measures the excess or shortfall of cash flows, in present value terms, once financing charges are met.
Cash flow	Cash flow refers to the movement of cash into or out of a business, a project, finite period of time. Measurement of Cash flow can be used
	· to determine a project"s rate of return or value. The time of Cash flows into and out of projects are used as inputs in financial models such as internal rate of return, and net present value. · to determine problems with a business"s liquidity.
Discounted cash flow	In finance, the Discounted cash flow approach describes a method of valuing a project, company, that reflects the risk of the cashflows.
Financial statements	financial statements (or financial reports) are formal records of the financial activities of a business, person, including United Kingdom company law, financial statements are often referred to as accounts, although the term financial statements is also used, particularly by accountants.
	financial statements provide an overview of a business or person"s financial condition in both short and long term.
Information technology	Information technology , as defined by the Information technology Association of America (ITAA), is "the study, design, development, implementation, support or management of computer-based information systems, particularly software applications and computer hardware." Information technology deals with the use of electronic computers and computer software to convert, store, protect, process, transmit, and securely retrieve information.
	Today, the term Information technology has ballooned to encompass many aspects of computing and technology, and the term has become very recognizable. Information technology professionals perform a variety of duties that range from installing applications to designing complex computer networks and information databases.
Intangible assets	intangible assets are defined as identifiable non-monetary assets that cannot be seen, touched or physically measured, which are created through time and/or effort and that are identifiable as a separate asset. There are two primary forms of intangibles - legal intangibles (such as trade secrets (e.g., customer lists), copyrights, patents, trademarks, and goodwill) and competitive intangibles (such as knowledge activities (know-how, knowledge), collaboration activities, leverage activities, and structural activities). Legal intangibles are known under the generic term intellectual property and generate legal property rights defensible in a court of law.
Adjustment	Adjustment means regulating, adapting or settling in a variety of contexts:
	Adjustment has several meanings; many relate to insurance, contracts, or the resolution of disputes.
	In Engineering, Mathematics and Geodesy, Adjustment means the optimal parameter estimation of a mathematical model so as to best fit a data set. The most important method is the least squares Adjustment, found by Carl Friedrich Gauss.

Chapter 7. Making Investment Decisions with the Net Present Value Rule

Chapter 7. Making Investment Decisions with the Net Present Value Rule

Asset

In business and accounting, Assets are economic resources owned by business or company. Anything tangible or intangible that one possesses, usually considered as applicable to the payment of one"s debts is considered an Asset. Simplistically stated, Assets are things of value that can be readily converted into cash (although cash itself is also considered an Asset).

Investment

Investment or investing is a term with several closely-related meanings in business management, finance and economics, related to saving or deferring consumption. Investing is the active redirection of resources: from being consumed today, to creating benefits in the future; the use of assets to earn income or profit. An Investment is a choice by an individual or an organization such as a pension fund, after at least some careful analysis or thought, to place or lend money in a vehicle (e.g. property, stock securities, bonds) that has sufficiently low risk and provides the possibility of generating returns over a period of time.

Capital budgeting

Capital budgeting (or investment appraisal) is the planning process used to determine whether a firm"s long term investments such as new machinery, replacement machinery, new plants, new products, and research development projects are worth pursuing. It is budget for major capital, or investment, expenditures.

Many formal methods are used in Capital budgeting, including the techniques such as

· Accounting rate of return
· Net present value
· Profitability index
· Internal rate of return
· Modified Internal Rate of Return
· Equivalent annuity

These methods use the incremental cash flows from each potential investment, or project Techniques based on accounting earnings and accounting rules are sometimes used - though economists consider this to be improper - such as the accounting rate of return, and "return on investment." Simplified and hybrid methods are used as well, such as payback period and discounted payback period.

Each potential project"s value should be estimated using a discounted cash flow (DCF) valuation, to find its net present value (NPV).

Rationing

Rationing is the controlled distribution of resources and scarce goods or services. Rationing controls the size of the ration, one"s allotted portion of the resources being distributed on a particular day or at a particular time.

In economics, it is often common to use the word "Rationing" to refer to one of the roles that prices play in markets, while Rationing (as the word is usually used) is called "non-price Rationing".

Discount rate

The Discount rate is an interest rate a central bank charges depository institutions that borrow reserves from it.

The term Discount rate has two meanings:

· the same as interest rate; the term "discount" does not refer to the meaning of the word, but to the purpose of using the quantity, such as computations of present value, e.g. net present value or discounted cash flow

· the annual effective Discount rate, which is the annual interest divided by the capital including that interest; this rate is lower than the interest rate; it corresponds to using the value after a year as the nominal value, and seeing the initial value as the nominal value minus a discount; it is used for Treasury Bills and similar financial instruments

Chapter 7. Making Investment Decisions with the Net Present Value Rule

Chapter 7. Making Investment Decisions with the Net Present Value Rule

	The annual effective Discount rate is the annual interest divided by the capital including that interest, which is the interest rate divided by 100% plus the interest rate. It is the annual discount factor to be applied to the future cash flow, to find the discount, subtracted from a future value to find the value one year earlier. For example, suppose there is a government bond that sells for $95 and pays $100 in a year"s time.
Opportunity cost	Opportunity cost or economic opportunity loss is the value of the next best alternative forgone as the result of making a decision. Opportunity cost analysis is an important part of a company"s decision-making processes but is not treated as an actual cost in any financial statement. The next best thing that a person can engage in is referred to as the Opportunity cost of doing the best thing and ignoring the next best thing to be done.
Opportunity cost of capital	The opportunity cost of capital is the expected return forgone by bypassing of other potential investment activities for a given capital. It is a rate of return that investors could earn in financial markets. .

Chapter 7. Making Investment Decisions with the Net Present Value Rule

Chapter 7. Making Investment Decisions with the Net Present Value Rule

Pratt ' Whitney	IV class=dablink>Pratt, American engineer, of the Pratt ' Whitney aircraft engine company
	· Gary Pratt, English cricketer
	· Geronimo Pratt, Black Panther
	· Greg Pratt, fictional character from the TV series ER
	· Guy Pratt, British bassist
	· Hiram Pratt , American politician -- Buffalo, New York
	· Hodgson Pratt, British pacifist
	· Hugo Pratt, Italian cartoonist
	· Jane Pratt, American magazine editor
	· John Pratt, several people
	· Joseph Gaither Pratt (1910-1979), American psychologist/parapsychologist
	· Joseph Marmaduke Pratt (1891-1946), American politician
	· Judson Pratt (1916-2002), American actor
	· Keri Lynn Pratt, American actress
	· Kyla Pratt, American actress
	· Larry Pratt, American lobbyist
	· Larry Pratt (baseball), American baseball player in the 1910"s
	· Louise Pratt, Australian politician
	· Marvin Pratt, American politician
	· Mary Pratt, Canadian artist
	· Mary Louise Pratt, American comparative literature professor and literary theorist
	· Michael Pratt, several people
	· Nicole Pratt, Australian tennis player
	· Nolan Pratt, Canadian professional ice hockey player
	· Orson Pratt, Latter-day Saint leader, brother to Parley P. Pratt
	· Parley P. Pratt, Latter-day Saint leader and Mormon martyr, brother to Orson Pratt
	· Peter Pratt, British actor
	· Phil Pratt, Jamaican musician
	· Pratt Institute, New York School of Fine Arts
	· Renée Gill Pratt, New Orleans Councilmember
	· Rey Pratt, Latter-day Saint leader in Mexico
	· Richard Pratt (Australian businessman), Australian businessman
	· Richard Henry Pratt, American soldier and educator
	· Richard L. Pratt, Jr., American Calvinist theologian and author
	· Robert and Henry Pratt, Canadian settlers
	· Roger Pratt, English architect of the seventeenth century
	· Sharon Pratt Kelly, American politician
	· Susan Pratt, American actress
	· Susan May Pratt, American actress
	· Theodore Pratt, American novelist
	· Thomas Pratt, American lawyer and politician
	· Thomas Willis Pratt, engineer, and father Caleb, architect, American inventors of the Pratt truss bridge design
	· Tim Pratt, American science fiction and fantasy writer and poet
	· Todd Pratt, Major League Baseball catcher
	· Vaughan Pratt, computer scientist (co-creator of the Knuth-Morris-Pratt algorithm)
	· Victoria Pratt, Canadian actress
	· Wallace Pratt, American geologist
	· William Henry Pratt, given name of actor Boris Karloff
	· William V. Pratt, American admiral
	· Zadock Pratt, US congressman and founder of Prattsville, New York .

Chapter 7. Making Investment Decisions with the Net Present Value Rule

Chapter 7. Making Investment Decisions with the Net Present Value Rule

Working capital	working Capital is a financial metric which represents operating liquidity available to a business. Along with fixed assets such as plant and equipment, working Capital is considered a part of operating capital. It is calculated as current assets minus current liabilities.
Consumer	consumer is a broad label that refers to any individuals or households that use goods and services generated within the economy. The concept of a consumer is used in different contexts, so that the usage and significance of the term may vary.
	Typically when business people and economists talk of consumers they are talking about person as consumer, an aggregated commodity item with little individuality other than that expressed in the buy/not-buy decision.
Consumer Price Index	A Consumer price index is a measure estimating the average price of consumer goods and services purchased by households. A Consumer price index measures a price change for a constant market basket of goods and services from one period to the next within the same area (city, region, or nation). It is a price index determined by measuring the price of a standard group of goods meant to represent the typical market basket of a typical urban consumer.
Monte Carlo methods	Monte Carlo methods are a class of computational algorithms that rely on repeated random sampling to compute their results. Monte Carlo methods are often used when simulating physical and mathematical systems. Because of their reliance on repeated computation of random or pseudo-random numbers, Monte Carlo methods are most suited to calculation by a computer.
Sunk costs	In economics and business decision-making, Sunk costs are retrospective (past) costs which have already been incurred and cannot be recovered. Sunk costs are sometimes contrasted with prospective costs which are future costs that may be incurred or changed if an action is taken. Both retrospective and prospective costs may be either fixed (that is, they are not dependent on the volume of economic activity, however measured) or variable (dependent on volume).
Inflation	In economics, Inflation is a rise in the general level of prices of goods and services in an economy over a period of time. When the price level rises, each unit of currency buys fewer goods and services; consequently, Inflation is also an erosion in the purchasing power of money - a loss of real value in the internal medium of exchange and unit of account in the economy. A chief measure of price Inflation is the Inflation rate, the annualized percentage change in a general price index (normally the Consumer Price Index) over time.
Interest	In the Renaissance era, greater mobility of people facilitated an increase in commerce and the appearance of appropriate conditions for entrepreneurs to start new, lucrative businesses. Given that borrowed money was no longer strictly for consumption but for production as well, Interest was no longer viewed in the same manner. The School of Salamanca elaborated on various reasons that justified the charging of Interest: the person who received a loan benefited, and one could consider Interest as a premium paid for the risk taken by the loaning party.
Interest rates	An interest rate is the price a borrower pays for the use of money they do not own, for instance a small company might borrow from a bank to kick start their business, and the return a lender receives for deferring the use of funds, by lending it to the borrower. Interest rates are normally expressed as a percentage rate over the period of one year.
	Interest rates targets are also a vital tool of monetary policy and are used to control variables like investment, inflation, and unemployment.

Chapter 7. Making Investment Decisions with the Net Present Value Rule

Chapter 7. Making Investment Decisions with the Net Present Value Rule

Nominal interest rate — In finance and economics Nominal interest rate or nominal rate of interest refers to the rate of interest before adjustment for inflation (in contrast with the real interest rate); or, for interest rates "as stated" without adjustment for the full effect of compounding (also referred to as the nominal annual rate). An interest rate is called nominal if the frequency of compounding (e.g. a month) is not identical to the basic time unit (normally a year).

The real interest rate includes compensation for the lender''s lost value due to inflation, whereas the Nominal interest rate excludes inflation.

Depreciation — Composite life equals the total Depreciable Cost divided by the total depreciation Per Year. $5,900 / $1,300 = 4.5 years.

Composite depreciation Rate equals depreciation Per Year divided by total Historical Cost.

Income statement — Income statement, also called profit and loss statement (P'L) and Statement of Operations, is a company''s financial statement that indicates how the revenue (money received from the sale of products and services before expenses are taken out, also known as the "top line") is transformed into the net income (the result after all revenues and expenses have been accounted for, also known as the "bottom line"). The purpose of the income statement is to show managers and investors whether the company made or lost money during the period being reported.

The important thing to remember about an income statement is that it represents a period of time.

Stock split — A Stock split or stock divide increases or decreases the number of shares in a public company. The price is adjusted such that the market capitalization of the company remains the same after the split, so that dilution does not occur. Options and warrants are included.

Dividend — Dividends are payments made by a corporation to its shareholder members. It is the portion of corporate profits paid out to stockholders. When a corporation earns a profit or surplus, that money can be put to two uses: it can either be re-invested in the business (called retained earnings), or it can be paid to the shareholders as a Dividend.

Forecasting — forecasting is the process of estimation in unknown situations. Prediction is a similar, but more general term. Both can refer to estimation of time series, cross-sectional or longitudinal data.

Investment decisions — Investment decisions are made by investors and investment managers.

Investors commonly perform investment analysis by making use of fundamental analysis, technical analysis and gut feel.

Investment decisions are often supported by decision tools.

Correlation swap — A Correlation swap is an over-the-counter financial derivative that allows one to speculate on or hedge risks associated with the observed average correlation, of a collection of underlying products, where each product has periodically observable prices, as with a commodity, exchange rate, interest rate, while the floating leg pays the annualized realized correlation $\rho_{realized}$. The contract value at expiration from the pay-fixed perspective is therefore

$N_{corr}(\rho_{realized} - \rho_{strike})$

Given a set of nonnegative weights w_i on n securities, with observed pairwise correlations measured to be $\rho_{i,j}$ the weighted average correlation is defined as

$$\rho_{realized} = \frac{\sum_{i,j} w_i w_j \rho_{i,j}}{\sum_{i,j} w_i w_j}$$

Chapter 7. Making Investment Decisions with the Net Present Value Rule

	No industry-standard models yet exist that have stochastic correlation and are arbitrage-free.
Capital structure	In finance, Capital structure refers to the way a corporation finances its assets through some combination of equity, debt, a firm that sells $20 billion in equity and $80 billion in debt is said to be 20% equity-financed and 80% debt-financed.
Debt	Debt is that which is owed; usually referencing assets owed, but the term can also cover moral obligations and other interactions not requiring money. In the case of assets, Debt is a means of using future purchasing power in the present before a summation has been earned. Some companies and corporations use Debt as a part of their overall corporate finance strategy.
Efficient-market hypothesis	In finance, the Efficient-market hypothesis (EMH) asserts that financial markets are "informationally efficient", stocks, bonds, or property) already reflect all known information, and instantly change to reflect new information. Therefore, according to theory, it is impossible to consistently outperform the market by using any information that the market already knows, except through luck. Information or news in the EMH is defined as anything that may affect prices that is unknowable in the present and thus appears randomly in the future.
Equity	Equity, in finance and accounting, refers to the residual claim or interest of the most junior class of investors in an asset, after all liabilities are paid. If valuations placed on assets do not exceed liabilities, negative Equity exists. In an accounting context, Shareholders" Equity (or stockholders" Equity, shareholders" funds, shareholders" capital or similar terms) represents the remaining interest in assets of a company, spread among individual shareholders of common or preferred stock.
Inventory	inventory is a list for goods and materials, held available in stock by a business. It is also used for a list of the contents of a household and for a list for testamentary purposes of the possessions of someone who has died. In accounting inventory is considered an asset.
Adjusted present value	Adjusted present value is a business valuation method. Adjusted present value is the net present value of a project if financed solely by ownership equity plus the present value of all the benefits of financing. It was first studied by Stewart Myers, a professor at the MIT Sloan School of Management and later theorized by Lorenzo Peccati, professor at the Bocconi University, in 1973.
	The method is to calculate the NPV of the project as if it is all-equity financed (so called base case).
Valuation	In finance, valuation is the process of estimating the potential market value of a financial asset or liability. valuations can be done on assets (for example, investments in marketable securities such as stocks, options, business enterprises, or intangible assets such as patents and trademarks) or on liabilities (e.g., Bonds issued by a company). valuations are required in many contexts including investment analysis, capital budgeting, merger and acquisition transactions, financial reporting, taxable events to determine the proper tax liability, and in litigation.
	valuation of financial assets is done using one or more of these types of models:

Chapter 7. Making Investment Decisions with the Net Present Value Rule

Chapter 7. Making Investment Decisions with the Net Present Value Rule

· Discounted Cash Flows determine the value by estimating the expected future earnings from owning the asset discounted to their present value.
· Relative value models determine the value based on the market prices of similar assets.
· Option pricing models are used for certain types of financial assets (e.g., warrants, put options, call options, employee stock options, investments with embedded options such as a callable bond) and are a complex present value model.

Value investing

Value investing is an investment paradigm that derives from the ideas on investment and speculation that Ben Graham ' David Dodd began teaching at Columbia Business School in 1928 and subsequently developed in their 1934 text Security Analysis. Although Value investing has taken many forms since its inception, it generally involves buying securities whose shares appear underpriced by some form(s) of fundamental analysis. As examples, such securities may be stock in public companies that trade at discounts to book value or tangible book value, have high dividend yields, have low price-to-earning multiples or have low price-to-book ratios.

Accounts payable

Accounts payable is a file or account that contains money that a person or company owes to suppliers, but has not paid yet (a form of debt). When you receive an invoice you add it to the file, and then you remove it when you pay. Thus, the A/P is a form of credit that suppliers offer to their purchasers by allowing them to pay for a product or service after it has already been received.

Accounts receivable

Accounts receivable (A/R) is one of a series of accounting transactions dealing with the billing of customers who owe money to a person, company or organization for goods and services that have been provided to the customer. In most business entities this is typically done by generating an invoice and mailing or electronically delivering it to the customer, who in turn must pay it within an established timeframe called credit or payment terms.

An example of a common payment term is Net 30, which means payment is due in the amount of the invoice 30 days from the date of invoice.

Accelerated depreciation

Accelerated depreciation refers to any one of several methods by which a company, for "financial accounting" and/or tax purposes, depreciates a fixed asset in such a way that the amount of depreciation taken each year is higher during the earlier years of an asset"s life. For financial accounting purposes, Accelerated depreciation is generally used when an asset is expected to be much more productive during its early years, so that depreciation expense will more accurately represent how much of an asset"s usefulness is being used up each year. For tax purposes, Accelerated depreciation provides a way of deferring corporate income taxes by reducing taxable income in current years, in exchange for increased taxable income in future years.

Tax

For similar words, see Taxi

To Tax is to impose a financial charge or other levy upon a Taxpayer (an individual or legal entity) by a state or the functional equivalent of a state such that failure to pay is punishable by law.

Taxes are also imposed by many subnational entities. Taxes consist of direct Tax or indirect Tax, and may be paid in money or as its labour equivalent (often but not always unpaid).

Tax shield

A Tax shield is the reduction in income taxes that results from taking an allowable deduction from taxable income. For example, because interest on debt is a tax-deductible expense, taking on debt creates a Tax shield. Since a Tax shield is a way to save cash flows, it increases the value of the business, and it is an important aspect of business valuation.

Chapter 7. Making Investment Decisions with the Net Present Value Rule

Deferred	deferred, in accrual accounting, is any account where the asset or liability is not realized until a future date (accounting period), e.g. annuities, charges, taxes, income, etc. The deferred item may be carried, dependent on type of deferral, as either an asset or liability.
Extreme value	The largest and the smallest element of a set are called extreme values, absolute extrema, extreme records, or optima. For a differentiable function f, if $f(x_0)$ is an extreme value for the set of all values $f(x)$, and if x_0 is in the interior of the domain of f, then x_0 is a critical point, by Fermat''s theorem.
	The point or points at which a function assumes its maximum (respectively, minimum) value are called the arg max (respectively, arg min): the arguments (inputs) at which the maximum (respectively, minimum) occurs.
Equivalent annual cost	In finance the Equivalent annual cost is the cost per year of owning and operating an asset over its entire lifespan.
	Equivalent annual cost is often used as a decision making tool in capital budgeting when comparing investment projects of unequal lifespans. For example if project A has an expected lifetime of 7 years, and project B has an expected lifetime of 11 years it would be improper to simply compare the net present values (NPVs) of the two projects, unless neither project could be repeated.
Technological change	technological change is a term that is used to describe the overall process of invention, innovation and diffusion of technology or processes. The term is redundant with technological development, technological achievement, and technological progress. In essence technological change is the invention of a technology (or a process), the continuous process of improving a technology (in which it often becomes cheaper) and its diffusion throughout industry or society.

Chapter 7. Making Investment Decisions with the Net Present Value Rule

Chapter 8. Introduction to Risk, Return, and the Opportunity Cost of Capital

Bond valuation	Bond valuation is the process of determining the fair price of a bond. As with any security or capital investment, the fair value of a bond is the present value of the stream of cash flows it is expected to generate. Hence, the value of a bond is determined by discounting the bond"s expected cash flows to the present using the appropriate discount rate.
Capital market	A Capital market is a market for securities (both debt and equity), where business enterprises (companies) and governments can raise long-term funds. It is defined as a market in which money is lent for periods longer than a year, as the raising of short-term funds takes place on other markets (e.g., the money market). The Capital market includes the stock market (equity securities) and the bond market (debt).
Common stock	Common stock is a form of corporate equity ownership, a type of security. It is called "common" to distinguish it from preferred stock. In the event of bankruptcy, Common stock investors receive their funds after preferred stock holders, bondholders, creditors, etc.
Dividend	Dividends are payments made by a corporation to its shareholder members. It is the portion of corporate profits paid out to stockholders. When a corporation earns a profit or surplus, that money can be put to two uses: it can either be re-invested in the business (called retained earnings), or it can be paid to the shareholders as a Dividend.
Equity	Equity, in finance and accounting, refers to the residual claim or interest of the most junior class of investors in an asset, after all liabilities are paid. If valuations placed on assets do not exceed liabilities, negative Equity exists. In an accounting context, Shareholders" Equity (or stockholders" Equity, shareholders" funds, shareholders" capital or similar terms) represents the remaining interest in assets of a company, spread among individual shareholders of common or preferred stock.
Market risk	Market risk is the risk that the value of an investment will decrease due to moves in market factors. The four standard Market risk factors are: · Equity risk, the risk that stock prices will change. · Interest rate risk, the risk that interest rates will change. · Currency risk, the risk that foreign exchange rates will change. · Commodity risk, the risk that commodity prices (e.g. corn, copper, crude oil) will change. As with other forms of risk, Market risk may be measured in a number of ways. Traditionally, this is done using a Value at Risk methodology.
Rate of return	Yield is the compound Rate of return that includes the effect of reinvesting interest or dividends. To the right is an example of a stock investment of one share purchased at the beginning of the year for $100. · The quarterly dividend is reinvested at the quarter-end stock price. · The number of shares purchased each quarter = ($ Dividend)/($ Stock Price). · The final investment value of $103.02 is a 3.02% Yield on the initial investment of $100. This is the compound yield, and this return can be considered to be the return on the investment of $100. To calculate the Rate of return, the investor includes the reinvested dividends in the total investment. The investor received a total of $4.06 in dividends over the year, all of which were reinvested, so the investment amount increased by $4.06.

Chapter 8. Introduction to Risk, Return, and the Opportunity Cost of Capital

- Total Investment = Cost Basis = $100 + $4.06 = $104.06.
- Capital gain/loss = $103.02 - $104.06 = -$1.04 (a capital loss)
- ($4.06 dividends - $1.04 capital loss) / $104.06 total investment = 2.9% ROI

The disadvantage of this ROI calculation is that it does not take into account the fact that not all the money was invested during the entire year (the dividend reinvestments occurred throughout the year).

Correlation swap

A Correlation swap is an over-the-counter financial derivative that allows one to speculate on or hedge risks associated with the observed average correlation, of a collection of underlying products, where each product has periodically observable prices, as with a commodity, exchange rate, interest rate, while the floating leg pays the annualized realized correlation $\rho_{realized}$. The contract value at expiration from the pay-fixed perspective is therefore

$N_{corr}(\rho_{realized} - \rho_{strike})$

Given a set of nonnegative weights w_i on n securities, with observed pairwise correlations measured to be $\rho_{i,j}$ the weighted average correlation is defined as

$$\rho_{realized} = \frac{\sum_{i,j} w_i w_j \rho_{i,j}}{\sum_{i,j} w_i w_j}$$

No industry-standard models yet exist that have stochastic correlation and are arbitrage-free.

Treasury bonds

A United States Treasury security is a government debt issued by the United States Department of the Treasury through the Bureau of the Public Debt. Treasury securities are the debt financing instruments of the United States Federal government, and they are often referred to simply as Treasuries. There are four types of marketable treasury securities: Treasury bills, Treasury notes, treasury Bonds, and Treasury Inflation Protected Securities (TIPS).

Risk premium

A Risk premium is the minimum difference a person requires to be willing to take an uncertain bet, between the expected value of the bet and the certain value that he is indifferent to.

The certainty equivalent is the guaranteed payoff at which a person is "indifferent" between accepting the guaranteed payoff and a higher but uncertain payoff. (It is the amount of the higher payout minus the Risk premium).

Cost

In business, retail, and accounting, a cost is the value of money that has been used up to produce something, and hence is not available for use anymore. In economics, a cost is an alternative that is given up as a result of a decision. In business, the cost may be one of acquisition, in which case the amount of money expended to acquire it is counted as cost.

Cost of capital

In business and finance, the cost of capital is the cost of obtaining funds for, or, conversely, the required return necessary to meet its cost of financing a capital budgeting project. Said another way, it is "the minimum return that a company should make on its own investments, to earn the cash flow out of which investors can be paid their return." cost of capital encompasses the two fundamental sources of financing: the cost of debt (including bonds and loans) and the cost of equity.

Capital (money) used for funding a business should earn returns for the capital providers who risk their capital.

Market portfolio

A Market portfolio is a portfolio consisting of a weighted sum of every asset in the market, with weights in the proportions that they exist in the market (with the necessary assumption that these assets are infinitely divisible).

Chapter 8. Introduction to Risk, Return, and the Opportunity Cost of Capital

Chapter 8. Introduction to Risk, Return, and the Opportunity Cost of Capital

	Neha Tyagi"s critique (1977) states that this is only a theoretical concept, as to create a Market portfolio for investment purposes in practice would necessarily include every single possible available asset, including real estate, precious metals, stamp collections, jewelry, and anything with any worth, as the theoretical market being referred to would be the world market. As a result, proxies for the market are used in practice by investors.
Dividend yield	The Dividend yield or the dividend-price ratio on a company stock is the company"s annual dividend payments divided by its market cap
Depression	In economics, a depression is a sustained, long-term downturn in economic activity in one or more economies. It is a more severe downturn than a recession, which is seen as part of a normal business cycle.
	Considered a rare and extreme form of recession, a depression is characterized by its length, and by abnormal increases in unemployment, falls in the availability of credit, shrinking output and investment, numerous bankruptcies, reduced amounts of trade and commerce, as well as highly volatile relative currency value fluctuations, mostly devaluations.
Great Depression	The Great Depression was a severe worldwide economic depression in the decade preceding World War II. The timing of the Great Depression varied across nations, but in most countries it started in about 1929 and lasted until the late 1930s or early 1940s. It was the longest, most widespread, and deepest depression of the 20th century, and is used in the 21st century as an example of how far the world"s economy can decline. The depression originated in the United States, triggered by the stock market crash of October 29, 1929 (known as Black Tuesday), but quickly spread to almost every country in the world.
Portfolio theory	Modern portfolio theory (MPT) is a theory of investment which attempts to explain how investors can maximize return and minimize risk. Although MPT is widely used in practice in the financial industry and several of its creators won a Nobel prize for the theory, in recent years the basic assumptions of MPT have been widely challenged by fields such as behavioral economics, and many companies using variants of MPT have gone bankrupt in various financial crises.
	MPT is a mathematical formulation of the concept of diversification in investing, with the aim of selecting a collection of investment assets that has collectively lower risk than any individual asset.
Standard deviation	In probability theory and statistics, the Standard deviation of a statistical population, a data set, being algebraically more tractable though practically less robust than the expected deviation or average absolute deviation. A low Standard deviation indicates that the data points tend to be very close to the mean, whereas high Standard deviation indicates that the data are spread out over a large range of values.
Variance	In probability theory and statistics, the Variance of a random variable or distribution is the expected square deviation of that variable from its expected value or mean). For example, a perfect die, when thrown, has expected value 7/2, expected deviation 3/2 (the mean of the equally likely absolute deviations 1/2, 3/2, 5/2), but expected square deviation 35/12 ≈ 2.9 (the mean of the equally likely squared deviations 1/4, 9/4, and 25/4). As another example, the two roots of the quadratic $ax^2 + bx + c$ have mean the root of its derivative $2ax + b$, namely $x = -b/2a$, and Variance its discriminant $b^2 - 4ac$ divided by $4a^2$, this being the square deviation of each root from the mean.
Black Monday	Black Monday is a term used to refer to certain events which occur on a Monday. It has been used in the following cases:

Chapter 8. Introduction to Risk, Return, and the Opportunity Cost of Capital

· Black Monday, Dublin, 1209 - when a group of 500 recently arrived settlers from Bristol were massacred by warriors of the Gaelic O"Byrne clan. The group had left the safety of the walled city of Dublin to celebrate Easter Monday near a wood at Ranelagh, when they were attacked without warning. For centuries afterwards, this event was commemorated by a mustering of soldiers on the day as a challenge to the native tribes.
· Black Monday, 14 April 1360 - the army of Edward III during the Hundred Years" War was struck by hailstorms, lightning and panic, causing considerable loss of life on Easter Monday.
· Black Monday, 27 February 1865 - a "sirocco" wind brought sandstorms to Melbourne, Australia affecting Sandhurst and Castlemaine.
· Black Monday, 8 February 1886 - when a major protest over unemployment led to a riot in Pall Mall, London.
· Black Monday, December 10, 1894 - when both banks of Newfoundland, Britain"s oldest colony, had closed their doors, thus rendering that colony"s main medium of exchange worthless.
· Black Monday, 28 October 1929 - a day in the Wall Street Crash of 1929, which also saw major stock market upheaval.
· Black Monday, 27 May 1935 - US Supreme Court Justices overturned multiple Acts including National Industrial Recovery Act.
· Black Monday, September 19, 1977 - when Youngstown Sheet and Tube Company, one of America"s largest regional steel-manufacturing firms, announced that it would shut down most of its operations in the vicinity of Youngstown, Ohio.

Diversification

Diversification in finance is a risk management technique, related to hedging, that mixes a wide variety of investments within a portfolio. It is the spreading out investments to reduce risks. Because the fluctuations of a single security have less impact on a diverse portfolio, Diversification minimizes the risk from any one investment.

New York Stock Exchange

The New York Stock Exchange is a stock exchange located at 11 Wall Street in lower Manhattan, New York City, New York, USA. It is the largest stock exchange in the world by United States dollar value of its listed companies" securities. As of October 2008, the combined capitalization of all domestic New York Stock Exchange listed companies was US$10.1 trillion.

The New York Stock Exchange is operated by New York Stock Exchange Euronext, which was formed by the New York Stock Exchange "s 2007 merger with the fully-electronic stock exchange Euronext.

Covariance

In probability theory and statistics, Covariance is a measure of how much two variables change together. (Variance is a special case of the Covariance when the two variables are identical).

If two variables tend to vary together (that is, when one of them is above its expected value, then the other variable tends to be above its expected value too), then the Covariance between the two variables will be positive.

Securities

A security is a fungible, negotiable instrument representing financial value. Securities are broadly categorized into debt Securities (such as banknotes, bonds and debentures); equity Securities, e.g., common stocks; and derivative contracts, such as forwards, futures, options and swaps. The company or other entity issuing the security is called the issuer.

Chapter 8. Introduction to Risk, Return, and the Opportunity Cost of Capital

Chapter 9. Risk and Return

Market risk

Market risk is the risk that the value of an investment will decrease due to moves in market factors. The four standard Market risk factors are:

· Equity risk, the risk that stock prices will change.
· Interest rate risk, the risk that interest rates will change.
· Currency risk, the risk that foreign exchange rates will change.
· Commodity risk, the risk that commodity prices (e.g. corn, copper, crude oil) will change.

As with other forms of risk, Market risk may be measured in a number of ways. Traditionally, this is done using a Value at Risk methodology.

Portfolio theory

Modern portfolio theory (MPT) is a theory of investment which attempts to explain how investors can maximize return and minimize risk. Although MPT is widely used in practice in the financial industry and several of its creators won a Nobel prize for the theory, in recent years the basic assumptions of MPT have been widely challenged by fields such as behavioral economics, and many companies using variants of MPT have gone bankrupt in various financial crises.

MPT is a mathematical formulation of the concept of diversification in investing, with the aim of selecting a collection of investment assets that has collectively lower risk than any individual asset.

Standard deviation

In probability theory and statistics, the Standard deviation of a statistical population, a data set, being algebraically more tractable though practically less robust than the expected deviation or average absolute deviation. A low Standard deviation indicates that the data points tend to be very close to the mean, whereas high Standard deviation indicates that the data are spread out over a large range of values.

Log-normal distribution

In probability theory, a log-normal distribution is a probability distribution of a random variable whose logarithm is normally distributed. If X is a random variable with a normal distribution, then Y = exp(X) has a log-normal distribution; likewise, if Y is log-normally distributed, then log(Y) is normally distributed. (The base of the logarithmic function does not matter: if $\log_a(Y)$ is normally distributed, then so is $\log_b(Y)$, for any two positive numbers a, b ≠ 1).

Linear programming

In mathematics, linear programming is a technique for optimization of a linear objective function, subject to linear equality and linear inequality constraints. Informally, linear programming determines the way to achieve the best outcome (such as maximum profit or lowest cost) in a given mathematical model and given some list of requirements represented as linear equations.

More formally, given a polytope (for example, a polygon or a polyhedron), and a real-valued affine function

$$f(x_1, x_2, \ldots, x_n) = c_1 x_1 + c_2 x_2 + \cdots + c_n x_n + d$$

defined on this polytope, a linear programming method will find a point in the polytope where this function has the smallest (or largest) value.

Rationing

Rationing is the controlled distribution of resources and scarce goods or services. Rationing controls the size of the ration, one"s allotted portion of the resources being distributed on a particular day or at a particular time.

In economics, it is often common to use the word "Rationing" to refer to one of the roles that prices play in markets, while Rationing (as the word is usually used) is called "non-price Rationing".

Chapter 9. Risk and Return

Debt — Debt is that which is owed; usually referencing assets owed, but the term can also cover moral obligations and other interactions not requiring money. In the case of assets, Debt is a means of using future purchasing power in the present before a summation has been earned. Some companies and corporations use Debt as a part of their overall corporate finance strategy.

Capital structure — In finance, Capital structure refers to the way a corporation finances its assets through some combination of equity, debt, a firm that sells $20 billion in equity and $80 billion in debt is said to be 20% equity-financed and 80% debt-financed.

Risk premium — A Risk premium is the minimum difference a person requires to be willing to take an uncertain bet, between the expected value of the bet and the certain value that he is indifferent to.

The certainty equivalent is the guaranteed payoff at which a person is "indifferent" between accepting the guaranteed payoff and a higher but uncertain payoff. (It is the amount of the higher payout minus the Risk premium).

Sharpe ratio — The Sharpe ratio or Sharpe index or Sharpe measure or reward-to-variability ratio is a measure of the excess return (or Risk Premium) per unit of risk in an investment asset or a trading strategy it is defined as:

$$S = \frac{R - R_f}{\sigma} = \frac{E[R - R_f]}{\sqrt{\mathrm{var}[R - R_f]}},$$

where R is the asset return, R_f is the return on a benchmark asset, such as the risk free rate of return, $E[R - R_f]$ is the expected value of the excess of the asset return over the benchmark return, and σ is the standard deviation of the asset excess return.

Note, if R_f is a constant risk free return throughout the period,

$$\sqrt{\mathrm{var}[R - R_f]} = \sqrt{\mathrm{var}[R]}.$$

The Sharpe ratio is used to characterize how well the return of an asset compensates the investor for the risk taken. When comparing two assets each with the expected return E[R] against the same benchmark with return R_f, the asset with the higher Sharpe ratio gives more return for the same risk.

Dividend — Dividends are payments made by a corporation to its shareholder members. It is the portion of corporate profits paid out to stockholders. When a corporation earns a profit or surplus, that money can be put to two uses: it can either be re-invested in the business (called retained earnings), or it can be paid to the shareholders as a Dividend.

Dividend yield — The Dividend yield or the dividend-price ratio on a company stock is the company"s annual dividend payments divided by its market cap

Return — Returns .

Capital asset — The term Capital asset has three unrelated technical definitions, and is also used in a variety of non-technical ways.

Chapter 9. Risk and Return

Chapter 9. Risk and Return

· In financial economics, it refers to any asset used to make money, as opposed to assets used for personal enjoyment or consumption. This is an important distinction because two people can disagree sharply about the value of personal assets, one person might think a sports car is more valuable than a pickup truck, another person might have the opposite taste. But if an asset is held for the purpose of making money, taste has nothing to do with it, only differences of opinion about how much money the asset will produce.

Capital asset pricing model

In finance, the Capital asset pricing model is used to determine a theoretically appropriate required rate of return of an asset, if that asset is to be added to an already well-diversified portfolio, given that asset''s non-diversifiable risk. The model takes into account the asset''s sensitivity to non-diversifiable risk (also known as systematic risk or market risk), often represented by the quantity beta (β) in the financial industry, as well as the expected return of the market and the expected return of a theoretical risk-free asset.

The model was introduced by Jack Treynor (1961, 1962), William Sharpe (1964), John Lintner (1965a,b) and Jan Mossin (1966) independently, building on the earlier work of Harry Markowitz on diversification and modern portfolio theory.

Capital market

A Capital market is a market for securities (both debt and equity), where business enterprises (companies) and governments can raise long-term funds. It is defined as a market in which money is lent for periods longer than a year, as the raising of short-term funds takes place on other markets (e.g., the money market). The Capital market includes the stock market (equity securities) and the bond market (debt).

Security market line

In Modern Portfolio Theory, the security market line is the graphical representation of the Capital Asset Pricing Model. It displays the expected rate of return for an overall market as a function of systematic, non-diversifiable risk (its beta).

The Y-Intercept (beta=0) of the security market line is equal to the risk-free interest rate.

Valuation

In finance, valuation is the process of estimating the potential market value of a financial asset or liability. valuations can be done on assets (for example, investments in marketable securities such as stocks, options, business enterprises, or intangible assets such as patents and trademarks) or on liabilities (e.g., Bonds issued by a company). valuations are required in many contexts including investment analysis, capital budgeting, merger and acquisition transactions, financial reporting, taxable events to determine the proper tax liability, and in litigation.

valuation of financial assets is done using one or more of these types of models:

· Discounted Cash Flows determine the value by estimating the expected future earnings from owning the asset discounted to their present value.
· Relative value models determine the value based on the market prices of similar assets.
· Option pricing models are used for certain types of financial assets (e.g., warrants, put options, call options, employee stock options, investments with embedded options such as a callable bond) and are a complex present value model.

Correlation swap

A Correlation swap is an over-the-counter financial derivative that allows one to speculate on or hedge risks associated with the observed average correlation, of a collection of underlying products, where each product has periodically observable prices, as with a commodity, exchange rate, interest rate, while the floating leg pays the annualized realized correlation $\rho_{realized}$. The contract value at expiration from the pay-fixed perspective is therefore

$N_{corr}(\rho_{realized} - \rho_{strike})$

Chapter 9. Risk and Return

Given a set of nonnegative weights w_i on n securities, with observed pairwise correlations measured to be $\rho_{i,j}$ the weighted average correlation is defined as

$$\rho_{\text{realized}} = \frac{\sum_{i,j} w_i w_j \rho_{i,j}}{\sum_{i,j} w_i w_j}$$

No industry-standard models yet exist that have stochastic correlation and are arbitrage-free.

Cost

In business, retail, and accounting, a cost is the value of money that has been used up to produce something, and hence is not available for use anymore. In economics, a cost is an alternative that is given up as a result of a decision. In business, the cost may be one of acquisition, in which case the amount of money expended to acquire it is counted as cost.

Cost of capital

In business and finance, the cost of capital is the cost of obtaining funds for, or, conversely, the required return necessary to meet its cost of financing a capital budgeting project. Said another way, it is "the minimum return that a company should make on its own investments, to earn the cash flow out of which investors can be paid their return." cost of capital encompasses the two fundamental sources of financing: the cost of debt (including bonds and loans) and the cost of equity.

Capital (money) used for funding a business should earn returns for the capital providers who risk their capital.

Market portfolio

A Market portfolio is a portfolio consisting of a weighted sum of every asset in the market, with weights in the proportions that they exist in the market (with the necessary assumption that these assets are infinitely divisible).

Neha Tyagi"s critique (1977) states that this is only a theoretical concept, as to create a Market portfolio for investment purposes in practice would necessarily include every single possible available asset, including real estate, precious metals, stamp collections, jewelry, and anything with any worth, as the theoretical market being referred to would be the world market. As a result, proxies for the market are used in practice by investors.

Capital budgeting

Capital budgeting (or investment appraisal) is the planning process used to determine whether a firm"s long term investments such as new machinery, replacement machinery, new plants, new products, and research development projects are worth pursuing. It is budget for major capital, or investment, expenditures.

Many formal methods are used in Capital budgeting, including the techniques such as

· Accounting rate of return
· Net present value
· Profitability index
· Internal rate of return
· Modified Internal Rate of Return
· Equivalent annuity

These methods use the incremental cash flows from each potential investment, or project Techniques based on accounting earnings and accounting rules are sometimes used - though economists consider this to be improper - such as the accounting rate of return, and "return on investment." Simplified and hybrid methods are used as well, such as payback period and discounted payback period.

Each potential project"s value should be estimated using a discounted cash flow (DCF) valuation, to find its net present value (NPV).

Chapter 9. Risk and Return

Chapter 9. Risk and Return

Net present value	Net present value or net present worth (NPW) is defined as the total present value (PV) of a time series of cash flows. It is a standard method for using the time value of money to appraise long-term projects. Used for capital budgeting, and widely throughout economics, it measures the excess or shortfall of cash flows, in present value terms, once financing charges are met.
Present value	Present value is the value on a given date of a future payment or series of future payments, discounted to reflect the time value of money and other factors such as investment risk. Present value calculations are widely used in business and economics to provide a means to compare cash flows at different times on a meaningful "like to like" basis.
	If offered a choice between $100 today or $100 in one year, a rational person will choose $100 today.
Price-to-book ratio	The price-to-book ratio, is a financial ratio used to compare a company''s book value to its current market price. Book value is an accounting term denoting the portion of the company held by the shareholders; in other words, the company''s total tangible assets less its total liabilities. The calculation can be performed in two ways, but the result should be the same each way.
Data snooping	In statistics, data-snooping bias is a form of statistical bias generated by the misuse of data mining techniques which can lead to bogus results in scientific research. Although data-snooping biases can occur in any field that uses data mining, Data snooping biases are a particular concern in finance and medical research, both of which make heavy use of data mining techniques.
	In the process of data mining, huge numbers of hypotheses about a single data set can be tested in a very short time, by exhaustively searching for combinations of variables that might show a correlation.
Growth stock	In finance, Growth stocks are stocks belonging to companies that have shown high growth (e.g. in earnings) in the past and, it is hoped, will continue to grow, leading to good investor returns.
	Analysts compute ROE by taking the company''s net income and dividing it by the company''s equity. To be classified as a Growth stock, analysts expect to see at least 15 percent return on equity.
Value Line	Value Line, Inc.(NASDAQ: VALU), is a New York corporation founded in 1931 by Arnold Bernhard, best known for publishing the The Value Line Investment Survey , a stock analysis newsletter that''s updated weekly and kept by subscribers in a large black or green binder. The survey itself is broken into three parts; Ratings ' Reports, Table of Summary ' Index Contents, and Selection ' Opinion.
	Value Line, in its current form, was incorporated in 1982 and is the successor to substantially all of the operations of Arnold Bernhard ' Co., Inc.
Fixed tax	A Fixed tax is a lump sum tax that is not measured as a percentage of the tax base (income, wealth). Fixed taxes like a poll tax or sin tax are often considered regressive, but could have progressive effects if applied to luxury goods and services.
	Since citizens share common roads, military protection, policing, and other government services, some argue that citizens should pay the same amount for basic infrastructure.

Chapter 9. Risk and Return

Chapter 9. Risk and Return

Consumption beta	In finance, Consumption beta refers to a concept in an asset pricing model where the reward-to-risk ratio of an asset is dependent not on its sensitivity (or beta coefficient) to overall market risk, as it is in the classical Capital Asset Pricing Model, but rather on its sensitivity to overall aggregate consumption. It was first proposed by Douglas Breeden in 1979. .
Arbitrage	In economics and finance, Arbitrage is the practice of taking advantage of a price differential between two or more markets: striking a combination of matching deals that capitalize upon the imbalance, the profit being the difference between the market prices. When used by academics, an Arbitrage is a transaction that involves no negative cash flow at any probabilistic or temporal state and a positive cash flow in at least one state; in simple terms, a risk-free profit. A person who engages in Arbitrage is called an Arbitrageur--such as a bank or brokerage firm.
Arbitrage pricing theory	Arbitrage pricing theory , in finance, is a general theory of asset pricing, that has become influential in the pricing of stocks.
	Arbitrage pricing theory holds that the expected return of a financial asset can be modeled as a linear function of various macro-economic factors or theoretical market indices, where sensitivity to changes in each factor is represented by a factor-specific beta coefficient. The model-derived rate of return will then be used to price the asset correctly - the asset price should equal the expected end of period price discounted at the rate implied by model.
Sensitivity analysis	sensitivity analysis is the study of how the variation (uncertainty) in the output of a mathematical model can be apportioned, qualitatively or quantitatively, to different sources of variation in the input of a model .
	In more general terms uncertainty and sensitivity analyses investigate the robustness of a study when the study includes some form of mathematical modelling. While uncertainty analysis studies the overall uncertainty in the conclusions of the study, sensitivity analysis tries to identify what source of uncertainty weights more on the study"s conclusions.

Chapter 10. Capital Budgeting and Risk

Capital budgeting	Capital budgeting (or investment appraisal) is the planning process used to determine whether a firm"s long term investments such as new machinery, replacement machinery, new plants, new products, and research development projects are worth pursuing. It is budget for major capital, or investment, expenditures. Many formal methods are used in Capital budgeting, including the techniques such as · Accounting rate of return · Net present value · Profitability index · Internal rate of return · Modified Internal Rate of Return · Equivalent annuity These methods use the incremental cash flows from each potential investment, or project Techniques based on accounting earnings and accounting rules are sometimes used - though economists consider this to be improper - such as the accounting rate of return, and "return on investment." Simplified and hybrid methods are used as well, such as payback period and discounted payback period. Each potential project"s value should be estimated using a discounted cash flow (DCF) valuation, to find its net present value (NPV).
Bank	A Bank is a financial institution licensed by a government. Its primary activities include borrowing and lending money. Many other financial activities were allowed over time.
Cost	In business, retail, and accounting, a cost is the value of money that has been used up to produce something, and hence is not available for use anymore. In economics, a cost is an alternative that is given up as a result of a decision. In business, the cost may be one of acquisition, in which case the amount of money expended to acquire it is counted as cost.
Cost of capital	In business and finance, the cost of capital is the cost of obtaining funds for, or, conversely, the required return necessary to meet its cost of financing a capital budgeting project. Said another way, it is "the minimum return that a company should make on its own investments, to earn the cash flow out of which investors can be paid their return." cost of capital encompasses the two fundamental sources of financing: the cost of debt (including bonds and loans) and the cost of equity. Capital (money) used for funding a business should earn returns for the capital providers who risk their capital.
Capital asset	The term Capital asset has three unrelated technical definitions, and is also used in a variety of non-technical ways. · In financial economics, it refers to any asset used to make money, as opposed to assets used for personal enjoyment or consumption. This is an important distinction because two people can disagree sharply about the value of personal assets, one person might think a sports car is more valuable than a pickup truck, another person might have the opposite taste. But if an asset is held for the purpose of making money, taste has nothing to do with it, only differences of opinion about how much money the asset will produce.
Capital asset pricing model	In finance, the Capital asset pricing model is used to determine a theoretically appropriate required rate of return of an asset, if that asset is to be added to an already well-diversified portfolio, given that asset"s non-diversifiable risk. The model takes into account the asset"s sensitivity to non-diversifiable risk (also known as systematic risk or market risk), often represented by the quantity beta (β) in the financial industry, as well as the expected return of the market and the expected return of a theoretical risk-free asset.

Chapter 10. Capital Budgeting and Risk

	The model was introduced by Jack Treynor (1961, 1962), William Sharpe (1964), John Lintner (1965a,b) and Jan Mossin (1966) independently, building on the earlier work of Harry Markowitz on diversification and modern portfolio theory.
Debt	Debt is that which is owed; usually referencing assets owed, but the term can also cover moral obligations and other interactions not requiring money. In the case of assets, Debt is a means of using future purchasing power in the present before a summation has been earned. Some companies and corporations use Debt as a part of their overall corporate finance strategy.
Valuation	In finance, valuation is the process of estimating the potential market value of a financial asset or liability. valuations can be done on assets (for example, investments in marketable securities such as stocks, options, business enterprises, or intangible assets such as patents and trademarks) or on liabilities (e.g., Bonds issued by a company). valuations are required in many contexts including investment analysis, capital budgeting, merger and acquisition transactions, financial reporting, taxable events to determine the proper tax liability, and in litigation.
	valuation of financial assets is done using one or more of these types of models:
	· Discounted Cash Flows determine the value by estimating the expected future earnings from owning the asset discounted to their present value.
	· Relative value models determine the value based on the market prices of similar assets.
	· Option pricing models are used for certain types of financial assets (e.g., warrants, put options, call options, employee stock options, investments with embedded options such as a callable bond) and are a complex present value model.
Capital structure	In finance, Capital structure refers to the way a corporation finances its assets through some combination of equity, debt, a firm that sells $20 billion in equity and $80 billion in debt is said to be 20% equity-financed and 80% debt-financed.
Cost of equity	In finance, the cost of equity is the minimum rate of return a firm must offer shareholders to compensate for waiting for their returns, and for bearing some risk.
	The cost of equity capital for a particular company is the rate of return on investment that is required by the company"s ordinary shareholders. The return consists both of dividend and capital gains, e.g. increases in the share price.
Equity	Equity, in finance and accounting, refers to the residual claim or interest of the most junior class of investors in an asset, after all liabilities are paid. If valuations placed on assets do not exceed liabilities, negative Equity exists. In an accounting context, Shareholders" Equity (or stockholders" Equity, shareholders" funds, shareholders" capital or similar terms) represents the remaining interest in assets of a company, spread among individual shareholders of common or preferred stock.
Return	Returns .
Santa Fe	Santa Fe or Santa Fé may be:
	Argentina:
	· Santa Fe, Argentina
	· Santa Fe Province

Chapter 10. Capital Budgeting and Risk

Brazil:

- Santa Fé, Paraná
- Santa Fé de Goiás
- Santa Fé de Minas (Minas Gerais)
- Santa Fé do Sul (São Paulo)
- Santa Fé do Araguaia (Tocantins)
- Bonito de Santa Fé (Paraíba)

Colombia:

- Santa Fe de Bogotá, also Santafé de Bogotá, former name of Bogotá, the nation"s capital
- Santa Fe de Ralito
- Santa Fe C.D.

Cuba:

- Santa Fe, Isle of Youth, on the Isle of Youth
- Santa Fe, Havana

Ecuador:

- Santa Fe Island, one of the Galápagos Islands

Honduras:

- Santa Fe, Colón
- Santa Fé, Ocotepeque

Mexico:

- Santa Fe, Baja California Sur
- Santa Fe, Chihuahua
- Santa Fe, Coahuila
- Santa Fe, Guanajuato
- Santa Fe, Jalisco
- Santa Fe (Mexico City), within Mexico City
- Santa Fe, Michoacán
- Santa Fe, Nayarit
- Santa Fe, Nuevo León
- Santa Fe, Sinaloa
- Santa Fe, Veracruz

Panama:

- Santa Fé, Veraguas
- Santa Fé, Darién

Philippines:

Chapter 10. Capital Budgeting and Risk

- Santa Fe, Cebu
- Santa Fe, Leyte
- Santa Fe, Nueva Vizcaya
- Santa Fe, Romblon

Spain:

- Santa Fe, Granada
- Santa Fe, Catalonia
- Santa Fe del Penedès (Catalonia)
- Santa Fe de Mondújar (Almería)

United States:

- Santa Fe, Florida
- Santa Fe, Indiana
- Santa Fe, Missouri
- Santa Fe, New Mexico, state capital of New Mexico
- Santa Fe, Ohio
- Santa Fe, Tennessee
- Santa Fe, Texas
- Santa Fe Springs, California
- Santa Fe County, New Mexico
- Rancho Santa Fe, California

Venezuela:

- Santa Fe, Falcón
- Santa Fe, Sucre

- Santa Fe de Nuevo México, a province of New Spain that existed from the late 16th century up through the early 19th century
- Santa Fe Trail, a historic 19th century transportation route across southwestern North America
- New Santa Fe Trail, an auto trail in the United States connecting Kansas City, Missouri with Los Angeles, California
- Lake Santa Fe, lake in northeastern Alachua County, Florida, USA
- Santa Fe River (Florida), a tributary of the Suwannee River, USA
- Santa Fe River (New Mexico), USA
- Santa Fe National Forest, a protected national forest in northern New Mexico in the southwestern United States.

- Santa Fe (group), a Cuban band
- Santa Fe (nude photo book), a title of Japanese actress Rie Miyazawa"s nude photo book
- Santa Fe Trail , a 1940 Western
- Santa Fe Passage, a 1955 American western movie
- Santa Fe (1951 film) a 1951 Western starring Randolph Scott
- Santa Fe (Jon Bon Jovi song), a song from the Jon Bon Jovi"s album Blaze of Glory

Chapter 10. Capital Budgeting and Risk

- Atchison, Topeka and Santa Fe Railway, often abbreviated as the "Santa Fe"
- Santa Fe de Luxe, the first extra-fare named passenger train on the Atchison, Topeka and Santa Fe Railway.

- Santa Fe Depot, original name of Union Station (San Diego), a train and bus terminus
- Hyundai Santa Fe, a sport utility vehicle
- USS Santa Fe, two US Navy ships named after Santa Fe, New Mexico
- ARA Santa Fe, multiple vessels in the Argentine navy

- Texas Santa Fe Expedition, an expedition to claim parts of northern New Mexico for Texas in 1841
- Santa Fe Natural Tobacco Company, a tobacco manufacturer
- Disney"s Hotel Santa Fe, a hotel at Disneyland Resort Paris
- Santa Fe College, in Gainesville, Florida, USA
- Santa Fe Community College, in Santa Fe, New Mexico, USA
- Santa Fe Institute - research of complex systems
- Santa Fé de Toloca, Spanish mission established within sight of the Santa Fe River in Florida, between 1606 and 1616 .

Asset	In business and accounting, Assets are economic resources owned by business or company. Anything tangible or intangible that one possesses, usually considered as applicable to the payment of one"s debts is considered an Asset. Simplistically stated, Assets are things of value that can be readily converted into cash (although cash itself is also considered an Asset).
Discount rate	The Discount rate is an interest rate a central bank charges depository institutions that borrow reserves from it. The term Discount rate has two meanings: · the same as interest rate; the term "discount" does not refer to the meaning of the word, but to the purpose of using the quantity, such as computations of present value, e.g. net present value or discounted cash flow · the annual effective Discount rate, which is the annual interest divided by the capital including that interest; this rate is lower than the interest rate; it corresponds to using the value after a year as the nominal value, and seeing the initial value as the nominal value minus a discount; it is used for Treasury Bills and similar financial instruments The annual effective Discount rate is the annual interest divided by the capital including that interest, which is the interest rate divided by 100% plus the interest rate. It is the annual discount factor to be applied to the future cash flow, to find the discount, subtracted from a future value to find the value one year earlier. For example, suppose there is a government bond that sells for $95 and pays $100 in a year"s time.
Opportunity cost	Opportunity cost or economic opportunity loss is the value of the next best alternative forgone as the result of making a decision. Opportunity cost analysis is an important part of a company"s decision-making processes but is not treated as an actual cost in any financial statement. The next best thing that a person can engage in is referred to as the Opportunity cost of doing the best thing and ignoring the next best thing to be done.

Chapter 10. Capital Budgeting and Risk

Opportunity cost of capital	The opportunity cost of capital is the expected return forgone by bypassing of other potential investment activities for a given capital. It is a rate of return that investors could earn in financial markets. .
Operating leverage	The Operating leverage is a measure of how revenue growth translates into growth in operating income. It is a measure of leverage, and of how risky (volatile) a company"s operating income is.
	There are various measures of Operating leverage, which can be interpreted analogously to financial leverage.
Cash flow	Cash flow refers to the movement of cash into or out of a business, a project, finite period of time. Measurement of Cash flow can be used
	· to determine a project"s rate of return or value. The time of Cash flows into and out of projects are used as inputs in financial models such as internal rate of return, and net present value.
	· to determine problems with a business"s liquidity.
Certainty equivalent	A risk premium is the minimum difference a person requires to be willing to take an uncertain bet, between the expected value of the bet and the certain value that he is indifferent to.
	The certainty equivalent is the guaranteed payoff at which a person is "indifferent" between accepting the guaranteed payoff and a higher but uncertain payoff. (It is the amount of the higher payout minus the risk premium).
Expected utility theorem	In economics, game theory, and decision theory the expected utility theorem or expected utility hypothesis predicts that the "betting preferences" of people with regard to uncertain outcomes (gambles) can be described by a mathematical relation which takes into account the size of a payout (whether in money or other goods), the probability of occurrence, risk aversion, and the different utility of the same payout to people with different assets or personal preferences. It is a more sophisticated theory than simply predicting that choices will be made based on expected value (which takes into account only the size of the payout and the probability of occurrence).
	Daniel Bernoulli described the complete theory in 1738. John von Neumann and Oskar Morgenstern reinterpreted and presented an axiomatization of the same theory in 1944. They proved that any "normal" preference relation over a finite set of states can be written as an expected utility, sometimes referred to as von Neumann-Morgenstern utility.
Discounted cash flow	In finance, the Discounted cash flow approach describes a method of valuing a project, company, that reflects the risk of the cashflows.
Common stock	Common stock is a form of corporate equity ownership, a type of security. It is called "common" to distinguish it from preferred stock. In the event of bankruptcy, Common stock investors receive their funds after preferred stock holders, bondholders, creditors, etc.
Rate of return	Yield is the compound Rate of return that includes the effect of reinvesting interest or dividends.
	To the right is an example of a stock investment of one share purchased at the beginning of the year for $100.
	· The quarterly dividend is reinvested at the quarter-end stock price.
	· The number of shares purchased each quarter = ($ Dividend)/($ Stock Price).
	· The final investment value of $103.02 is a 3.02% Yield on the initial investment of $100. This is the compound yield, and this return can be considered to be the return on the investment of $100.

Chapter 10. Capital Budgeting and Risk

Chapter 10. Capital Budgeting and Risk

To calculate the Rate of return, the investor includes the reinvested dividends in the total investment. The investor received a total of $4.06 in dividends over the year, all of which were reinvested, so the investment amount increased by $4.06.

· Total Investment = Cost Basis = $100 + $4.06 = $104.06.
· Capital gain/loss = $103.02 - $104.06 = -$1.04 (a capital loss)
· ($4.06 dividends - $1.04 capital loss) / $104.06 total investment = 2.9% ROI

The disadvantage of this ROI calculation is that it does not take into account the fact that not all the money was invested during the entire year (the dividend reinvestments occurred throughout the year).

Project finance

project finance is the long term financing of infrastructure and industrial projects based upon the projected cash flows of the project rather than the balance sheets of the project sponsors. Usually, a project financing structure involves a number of equity investors, known as sponsors, as well as a syndicate of banks that provide loans to the operation. The loans are most commonly non-recourse loans, which are secured by the project assets and paid entirely from project cash flow, rather than from the general assets or creditworthiness of the project sponsors, a decision in part supported by financial modeling.

Chapter 11. Project Analysis

Capital budgeting

Capital budgeting (or investment appraisal) is the planning process used to determine whether a firm"s long term investments such as new machinery, replacement machinery, new plants, new products, and research development projects are worth pursuing. It is budget for major capital, or investment, expenditures.

Many formal methods are used in Capital budgeting, including the techniques such as

- Accounting rate of return
- Net present value
- Profitability index
- Internal rate of return
- Modified Internal Rate of Return
- Equivalent annuity

These methods use the incremental cash flows from each potential investment, or project Techniques based on accounting earnings and accounting rules are sometimes used - though economists consider this to be improper - such as the accounting rate of return, and "return on investment." Simplified and hybrid methods are used as well, such as payback period and discounted payback period.

Each potential project"s value should be estimated using a discounted cash flow (DCF) valuation, to find its net present value (NPV).

Investment

Investment or investing is a term with several closely-related meanings in business management, finance and economics, related to saving or deferring consumption. Investing is the active redirection of resources: from being consumed today, to creating benefits in the future; the use of assets to earn income or profit. An Investment is a choice by an individual or an organization such as a pension fund, after at least some careful analysis or thought, to place or lend money in a vehicle (e.g. property, stock securities, bonds) that has sufficiently low risk and provides the possibility of generating returns over a period of time.

Investment decisions

Investment decisions are made by investors and investment managers.

Investors commonly perform investment analysis by making use of fundamental analysis, technical analysis and gut feel. Investment decisions are often supported by decision tools.

Monte Carlo methods

Monte Carlo methods are a class of computational algorithms that rely on repeated random sampling to compute their results. Monte Carlo methods are often used when simulating physical and mathematical systems. Because of their reliance on repeated computation of random or pseudo-random numbers, Monte Carlo methods are most suited to calculation by a computer.

Rate of return

Yield is the compound Rate of return that includes the effect of reinvesting interest or dividends.

To the right is an example of a stock investment of one share purchased at the beginning of the year for $100.

- The quarterly dividend is reinvested at the quarter-end stock price.
- The number of shares purchased each quarter = ($ Dividend)/($ Stock Price).
- The final investment value of $103.02 is a 3.02% Yield on the initial investment of $100. This is the compound yield, and this return can be considered to be the return on the investment of $100.

To calculate the Rate of return, the investor includes the reinvested dividends in the total investment. The investor received a total of $4.06 in dividends over the year, all of which were reinvested, so the investment amount increased by $4.06.

Chapter 11. Project Analysis

Chapter 11. Project Analysis

- Total Investment = Cost Basis = $100 + $4.06 = $104.06.
- Capital gain/loss = $103.02 - $104.06 = -$1.04 (a capital loss)
- ($4.06 dividends - $1.04 capital loss) / $104.06 total investment = 2.9% ROI

The disadvantage of this ROI calculation is that it does not take into account the fact that not all the money was invested during the entire year (the dividend reinvestments occurred throughout the year).

Sensitivity analysis	sensitivity analysis is the study of how the variation (uncertainty) in the output of a mathematical model can be apportioned, qualitatively or quantitatively, to different sources of variation in the input of a model .
	In more general terms uncertainty and sensitivity analyses investigate the robustness of a study when the study includes some form of mathematical modelling. While uncertainty analysis studies the overall uncertainty in the conclusions of the study, sensitivity analysis tries to identify what source of uncertainty weights more on the study"s conclusions.
Budget	The Budget of a government is a summary or plan of the intended revenues and expenditures of that government. The United States federal Budget is prepared by the Office of Management and Budget, and submitted to Congress for consideration. Invariably, Congress makes many and substantial changes.
Budget process	A budget process refers to the process by which governments create and approve a budget. Â· The Financial Service Department prepares worksheets to assist the department head in preparation of department budget estimates Â· The Administrator calls a meeting of managers and they present and discuss plans for the following year"s projected level of activity. Â· The managers can work with the Financial Services, or work alone to prepare an estimate for the departments coming year.
Break-even	In economics ' business, specifically cost accounting, the Break-even point (BEP) is the point at which cost or expenses and revenue are equal: there is no net loss or gain, and one has "broken even". A profit or a loss has not been made, although opportunity costs have been paid, and capital has received the risk-adjusted, expected return.
	For example, if a business sells less than 200 tables each month, it will make a loss, if it sells more, it will be a profit.
Scenario analysis	scenario analysis is a process of analyzing possible future events by considering alternative possible outcomes (scenarios).
	The analysis is designed to allow improved decision-making by allowing consideration of outcomes and their implications. scenario analysis can also be used to illuminate "wild cards." For example, analysis of the possibility of the earth being struck by a large celestial object (a meteor) suggests that whilst the probability is low, the damage inflicted is so high that the event is much more important (threatening) than the low probability (in any one year) alone would suggest.
Break-even point	In economics ' business, specifically cost accounting, the break-even point (BEP) is the point at which cost or expenses and revenue are equal: there is no net loss or gain, and one has "broken even". A profit or a loss has not been made, although opportunity costs have been paid, and capital has received the risk-adjusted, expected return.
	For example, if a business sells less than 200 tables each month, it will make a loss, if it sells more, it will be a profit.
Operating leverage	The Operating leverage is a measure of how revenue growth translates into growth in operating income. It is a measure of leverage, and of how risky (volatile) a company"s operating income is.

Chapter 11. Project Analysis

Chapter 11. Project Analysis

	There are various measures of Operating leverage, which can be interpreted analogously to financial leverage.
Asset	In business and accounting, Assets are economic resources owned by business or company. Anything tangible or intangible that one possesses, usually considered as applicable to the payment of one"s debts is considered an Asset. Simplistically stated, Assets are things of value that can be readily converted into cash (although cash itself is also considered an Asset).
Cash flow	Cash flow refers to the movement of cash into or out of a business, a project, finite period of time. Measurement of Cash flow can be used
	· to determine a project"s rate of return or value. The time of Cash flows into and out of projects are used as inputs in financial models such as internal rate of return, and net present value. · to determine problems with a business"s liquidity.
Discounted cash flow	In finance, the Discounted cash flow approach describes a method of valuing a project, company, that reflects the risk of the cashflows.
Net present value	Net present value or net present worth (NPW) is defined as the total present value (PV) of a time series of cash flows. It is a standard method for using the time value of money to appraise long-term projects. Used for capital budgeting, and widely throughout economics, it measures the excess or shortfall of cash flows, in present value terms, once financing charges are met.
Adjustment	Adjustment means regulating, adapting or settling in a variety of contexts:
	Adjustment has several meanings; many relate to insurance, contracts, or the resolution of disputes. In Engineering, Mathematics and Geodesy, Adjustment means the optimal parameter estimation of a mathematical model so as to best fit a data set. The most important method is the least squares Adjustment, found by Carl Friedrich Gauss.
Financial statements	financial statements (or financial reports) are formal records of the financial activities of a business, person, including United Kingdom company law, financial statements are often referred to as accounts, although the term financial statements is also used, particularly by accountants.
	financial statements provide an overview of a business or person"s financial condition in both short and long term.
Decision tree	A decision tree (or tree diagram) is a decision support tool that uses a tree-like graph or model of decisions and their possible consequences, including chance event outcomes, resource costs, and utility. decision trees are commonly used in operations research, specifically in decision analysis, to help identify a strategy most likely to reach a goal. Another use of decision trees is as a descriptive means for calculating conditional probabilities.
Present value	Present value is the value on a given date of a future payment or series of future payments, discounted to reflect the time value of money and other factors such as investment risk. Present value calculations are widely used in business and economics to provide a means to compare cash flows at different times on a meaningful "like to like" basis.
	If offered a choice between $100 today or $100 in one year, a rational person will choose $100 today.

Chapter 11. Project Analysis

Chapter 11. Project Analysis

Real option	In corporate finance, real options analysis or ROA applies put option and call option valuation techniques to capital budgeting decisions. A real option itself, is the right -- but not the obligation -- to undertake some business decision; typically the option to make, abandon, expand, or shrink a capital investment. For example, the opportunity to invest in the expansion of a firm"s factory, or alternatively to sell the factory, is a real option.

Chapter 12. Efficient Markets and Behavioral Finance

Debt	Debt is that which is owed; usually referencing assets owed, but the term can also cover moral obligations and other interactions not requiring money. In the case of assets, Debt is a means of using future purchasing power in the present before a summation has been earned. Some companies and corporations use Debt as a part of their overall corporate finance strategy.
Discount rate	The Discount rate is an interest rate a central bank charges depository institutions that borrow reserves from it. The term Discount rate has two meanings: · the same as interest rate; the term "discount" does not refer to the meaning of the word, but to the purpose of using the quantity, such as computations of present value, e.g. net present value or discounted cash flow · the annual effective Discount rate, which is the annual interest divided by the capital including that interest; this rate is lower than the interest rate; it corresponds to using the value after a year as the nominal value, and seeing the initial value as the nominal value minus a discount; it is used for Treasury Bills and similar financial instruments The annual effective Discount rate is the annual interest divided by the capital including that interest, which is the interest rate divided by 100% plus the interest rate. It is the annual discount factor to be applied to the future cash flow, to find the discount, subtracted from a future value to find the value one year earlier. For example, suppose there is a government bond that sells for $95 and pays $100 in a year"s time.
Net present value	Net present value or net present worth (NPW) is defined as the total present value (PV) of a time series of cash flows. It is a standard method for using the time value of money to appraise long-term projects. Used for capital budgeting, and widely throughout economics, it measures the excess or shortfall of cash flows, in present value terms, once financing charges are met.
Opportunity cost	Opportunity cost or economic opportunity loss is the value of the next best alternative forgone as the result of making a decision. Opportunity cost analysis is an important part of a company"s decision-making processes but is not treated as an actual cost in any financial statement. The next best thing that a person can engage in is referred to as the Opportunity cost of doing the best thing and ignoring the next best thing to be done.
Opportunity cost of capital	The opportunity cost of capital is the expected return forgone by bypassing of other potential investment activities for a given capital. It is a rate of return that investors could earn in financial markets. .
Present value	Present value is the value on a given date of a future payment or series of future payments, discounted to reflect the time value of money and other factors such as investment risk. Present value calculations are widely used in business and economics to provide a means to compare cash flows at different times on a meaningful "like to like" basis. If offered a choice between $100 today or $100 in one year, a rational person will choose $100 today.
Capital structure	In finance, Capital structure refers to the way a corporation finances its assets through some combination of equity, debt, a firm that sells $20 billion in equity and $80 billion in debt is said to be 20% equity-financed and 80% debt-financed.
Cash flow	Cash flow refers to the movement of cash into or out of a business, a project, finite period of time. Measurement of Cash flow can be used

Chapter 12. Efficient Markets and Behavioral Finance

Chapter 12. Efficient Markets and Behavioral Finance

	· to determine a project"s rate of return or value. The time of Cash flows into and out of projects are used as inputs in financial models such as internal rate of return, and net present value. · to determine problems with a business"s liquidity.
Efficient-market hypothesis	In finance, the Efficient-market hypothesis (EMH) asserts that financial markets are "informationally efficient", stocks, bonds, or property) already reflect all known information, and instantly change to reflect new information. Therefore, according to theory, it is impossible to consistently outperform the market by using any information that the market already knows, except through luck. Information or news in the EMH is defined as anything that may affect prices that is unknowable in the present and thus appears randomly in the future.
Equity	Equity, in finance and accounting, refers to the residual claim or interest of the most junior class of investors in an asset, after all liabilities are paid. If valuations placed on assets do not exceed liabilities, negative Equity exists. In an accounting context, Shareholders" Equity (or stockholders" Equity, shareholders" funds, shareholders" capital or similar terms) represents the remaining interest in assets of a company, spread among individual shareholders of common or preferred stock.
Investment	Investment or investing is a term with several closely-related meanings in business management, finance and economics, related to saving or deferring consumption. Investing is the active redirection of resources: from being consumed today, to creating benefits in the future; the use of assets to earn income or profit. An Investment is a choice by an individual or an organization such as a pension fund, after at least some careful analysis or thought, to place or lend money in a vehicle (e.g. property, stock securities, bonds) that has sufficiently low risk and provides the possibility of generating returns over a period of time.
Investment decisions	Investment decisions are made by investors and investment managers. Investors commonly perform investment analysis by making use of fundamental analysis, technical analysis and gut feel. Investment decisions are often supported by decision tools.
Monte Carlo methods	Monte Carlo methods are a class of computational algorithms that rely on repeated random sampling to compute their results. Monte Carlo methods are often used when simulating physical and mathematical systems. Because of their reliance on repeated computation of random or pseudo-random numbers, Monte Carlo methods are most suited to calculation by a computer.
Adjusted present value	Adjusted present value is a business valuation method. Adjusted present value is the net present value of a project if financed solely by ownership equity plus the present value of all the benefits of financing. It was first studied by Stewart Myers, a professor at the MIT Sloan School of Management and later theorized by Lorenzo Peccati, professor at the Bocconi University, in 1973. The method is to calculate the NPV of the project as if it is all-equity financed (so called base case).
Capital budgeting	Capital budgeting (or investment appraisal) is the planning process used to determine whether a firm"s long term investments such as new machinery, replacement machinery, new plants, new products, and research development projects are worth pursuing. It is budget for major capital, or investment, expenditures. Many formal methods are used in Capital budgeting, including the techniques such as

Chapter 12. Efficient Markets and Behavioral Finance

Chapter 12. Efficient Markets and Behavioral Finance

	· Accounting rate of return · Net present value · Profitability index · Internal rate of return · Modified Internal Rate of Return · Equivalent annuity These methods use the incremental cash flows from each potential investment, or project Techniques based on accounting earnings and accounting rules are sometimes used - though economists consider this to be improper - such as the accounting rate of return, and "return on investment." Simplified and hybrid methods are used as well, such as payback period and discounted payback period. Each potential project"s value should be estimated using a discounted cash flow (DCF) valuation, to find its net present value (NPV).
Value investing	Value investing is an investment paradigm that derives from the ideas on investment and speculation that Ben Graham ' David Dodd began teaching at Columbia Business School in 1928 and subsequently developed in their 1934 text Security Analysis. Although Value investing has taken many forms since its inception, it generally involves buying securities whose shares appear underpriced by some form(s) of fundamental analysis. As examples, such securities may be stock in public companies that trade at discounts to book value or tangible book value, have high dividend yields, have low price-to-earning multiples or have low price-to-book ratios.
Random walk	A Random walk is a mathematical formalization of a trajectory that consists of taking successive random steps. The results of Random walk analysis have been applied to computer science, physics, ecology, economics, and a number of other fields as a fundamental model for random processes in time. For example, the path traced by a molecule as it travels in a liquid or a gas, the search path of a foraging animal, the price of a fluctuating stock and the financial status of a gambler can all be modeled as Random walks.
Random walk hypothesis	The Random walk hypothesis is a financial theory stating that stock market prices evolve according to a random walk and thus the prices of the stock market cannot be predicted. It has been described as "jibing" with the efficient market hypothesis. Economists have historically accepted the Random walk hypothesis.
Abnormal return	In finance, an Abnormal return is the difference between the expected return of a security and the actual return. Abnormal returns are sometimes triggered by "events." Events can include mergers, dividend announcements, company earning announcements, interest rate increases, lawsuits, etc. all which can contribute to an Abnormal return.
Takeover	A reverse Takeover is a type of Takeover where a private company acquires a public company. This is usually done at the instigation of the larger, private company, the purpose being for the private company to effectively float itself while avoiding some of the expense and time involved in a conventional IPO. However, under AIM rules, a reverse take-over is an acquisition or acquisitions in a twelve month period which for an AIM company would:

Chapter 12. Efficient Markets and Behavioral Finance

Chapter 12. Efficient Markets and Behavioral Finance

· exceed 100% in any of the class tests; or
· result in a fundamental change in its business, board or voting control; or
· in the case of an investing company, depart substantially from the investing strategy stated in its admission document or, where no admission document was produced on admission, depart substantially from the investing strategy stated in its pre-admission announcement or, depart substantially from the investing strategy

Often a company acquiring another pays a specified amount for it. This money can be raised in a number of ways. Although the company may have sufficient funds available in its account, this is unusual.

Efficient market hypothesis	In finance, the efficient-market hypothesis asserts that financial markets are "informationally efficient", stocks, bonds, or property) already reflect all known information, and instantly change to reflect new information. Therefore, according to theory, it is impossible to consistently outperform the market by using any information that the market already knows, except through luck. Information or news in the Efficient market hypothesis is defined as anything that may affect prices that is unknowable in the present and thus appears randomly in the future.
Mutual fund	A Mutual fund is a professionally managed type of collective investment scheme that pools money from many investors and invests it in stocks, bonds, short-term money market instruments, and/or other securities. The Mutual fund will have a fund manager that trades the pooled money on a regular basis. The net proceeds or losses are then typically distributed to the investors annually.
Return	Returns .
Index fund	An Index fund or index tracker is a collective investment scheme (usually a mutual fund or exchange-traded fund) that aims to replicate the movements of an index of a specific financial market, regardless of market conditions. Tracking can be achieved by trying to hold all of the securities in the index, in the same proportions as the index. Other methods include statistically sampling the market and holding "representative" securities.
Capital asset	The term Capital asset has three unrelated technical definitions, and is also used in a variety of non-technical ways. · In financial economics, it refers to any asset used to make money, as opposed to assets used for personal enjoyment or consumption. This is an important distinction because two people can disagree sharply about the value of personal assets, one person might think a sports car is more valuable than a pickup truck, another person might have the opposite taste. But if an asset is held for the purpose of making money, taste has nothing to do with it, only differences of opinion about how much money the asset will produce.
Capital asset pricing model	In finance, the Capital asset pricing model is used to determine a theoretically appropriate required rate of return of an asset, if that asset is to be added to an already well-diversified portfolio, given that asset"s non-diversifiable risk. The model takes into account the asset"s sensitivity to non-diversifiable risk (also known as systematic risk or market risk), often represented by the quantity beta (β) in the financial industry, as well as the expected return of the market and the expected return of a theoretical risk-free asset.

Chapter 12. Efficient Markets and Behavioral Finance

Chapter 12. Efficient Markets and Behavioral Finance

The model was introduced by Jack Treynor (1961, 1962), William Sharpe (1964), John Lintner (1965a,b) and Jan Mossin (1966) independently, building on the earlier work of Harry Markowitz on diversification and modern portfolio theory.

Valuation

In finance, valuation is the process of estimating the potential market value of a financial asset or liability. valuations can be done on assets (for example, investments in marketable securities such as stocks, options, business enterprises, or intangible assets such as patents and trademarks) or on liabilities (e.g., Bonds issued by a company). valuations are required in many contexts including investment analysis, capital budgeting, merger and acquisition transactions, financial reporting, taxable events to determine the proper tax liability, and in litigation.

valuation of financial assets is done using one or more of these types of models:

· Discounted Cash Flows determine the value by estimating the expected future earnings from owning the asset discounted to their present value.
· Relative value models determine the value based on the market prices of similar assets.
· Option pricing models are used for certain types of financial assets (e.g., warrants, put options, call options, employee stock options, investments with embedded options such as a callable bond) and are a complex present value model.

Market anomaly

A Market anomaly (or inefficiency) is a price and/or return distortion on a financial market.

It is usually related to:

· either structural factors (unfair competition, lack of market transparency, ..).
· or behavioral biases by economic agents

It sometimes refers to phenomena contradicting the efficient market hypothesis. There are anomalies in relation to the economic fundamentals of the equity, technical trading rules, and economic calendar events.

Comprehensive income

Comprehensive income (or earnings) is a specific term used in companies" financial reporting from the company-whole point of view. Because that use excludes the effects of changing ownership interest, an economic measure of Comprehensive income is necessary for financial analysis from the shareholders" point of view

Comprehensive income is defined by the Financial Accounting Standards Board, or FASB, as "the change in equity [net assets] of a business enterprise during a period from transactions and other events and circumstances from nonowner sources. It includes all changes in equity during a period except those resulting from investments by owners and distributions to owners."

Comprehensive income is the sum of net income and other items that must bypass the income statement because they have not been realized, including items like an unrealized holding gain or loss from available for sale securities and foreign currency translation gains or losses.

Correlation swap

A Correlation swap is an over-the-counter financial derivative that allows one to speculate on or hedge risks associated with the observed average correlation, of a collection of underlying products, where each product has periodically observable prices, as with a commodity, exchange rate, interest rate, while the floating leg pays the annualized realized correlation $\rho_{realized}$. The contract value at expiration from the pay-fixed perspective is therefore

$N_{corr}(\rho_{realized} - \rho_{strike})$

Chapter 12. Efficient Markets and Behavioral Finance

Chapter 12. Efficient Markets and Behavioral Finance

Given a set of nonnegative weights w_i on n securities, with observed pairwise correlations measured to be $\rho_{i,j}$ the weighted average correlation is defined as

$$\rho_{\text{realized}} = \frac{\sum_{i,j} w_i w_j \rho_{i,j}}{\sum_{i,j} w_i w_j}$$

No industry-standard models yet exist that have stochastic correlation and are arbitrage-free.

Dividend

Dividends are payments made by a corporation to its shareholder members. It is the portion of corporate profits paid out to stockholders. When a corporation earns a profit or surplus, that money can be put to two uses: it can either be re-invested in the business (called retained earnings), or it can be paid to the shareholders as a Dividend.

Dividend payout ratio

Dividend payout ratio is the fraction of net income a firm pays to its stockholders in dividends:

$$\text{Dividend payout ratio} = \frac{\text{Dividends}}{\text{Net Income for the same period}}$$

The part of the earnings not paid to investors is left for investment to provide for future earnings growth. Investors seeking high current income and limited capital growth prefer companies with high Dividend payout ratio. However investors seeking capital growth may prefer lower payout ratio because capital gains are taxed at a lower rate.

Irrational exuberance

"Irrational Exuberance" is a phrase used by the then Federal Reserve Board Chairman, Alan Greenspan, in a speech given at the American Enterprise Institute during the stock market boom of the 1990s. The phrase was a warning that the market might be somewhat overvalued.

Greenspan"s comment was made on December 5, 1996 (emphasis added in excerpt):

The prescience of the short comment--not repeated by Greenspan since--within a rather dry and complex speech would not normally have been so memorable; however, it was followed by immediate slumps in stock markets worldwide, provoking a strong reaction in financial circles and making its way into colloquial speech.

Relative efficiency

In statistics, efficiency is a term used in the comparison of various statistical procedures and, in particular, it refers to a measure of the desirability of an estimator or of an experimental design. The relative efficiency of two procedures is the ratio their efficiencies, although often this term is used where the comparison is made between a given procedure and a notional "best possible" procedure. The efficiencies and the relative efficiency of two procedures theoretically depend on the sample size available for the given procedure, but it is often possible to use the asymptotic relative efficiency (defined as the limit of the relative efficiencies as the sample size grows) as the principal comparison measure.

Arbitrage

In economics and finance, Arbitrage is the practice of taking advantage of a price differential between two or more markets: striking a combination of matching deals that capitalize upon the imbalance, the profit being the difference between the market prices. When used by academics, an Arbitrage is a transaction that involves no negative cash flow at any probabilistic or temporal state and a positive cash flow in at least one state; in simple terms, a risk-free profit. A person who engages in Arbitrage is called an Arbitrageur--such as a bank or brokerage firm.

Chapter 12. Efficient Markets and Behavioral Finance

Short selling	In finance, short selling is the practice of selling assets, usually securities, that have been borrowed from a third party with the intention of buying identical assets back at a later date to return to the lender. The short seller hopes to profit from a decline in the price of the assets between the sale and the repurchase, as he will pay less to buy the assets than he received on selling them. Conversely, the short seller will make a loss if the price of the assets rises.
Finance	Finance is the science of funds management. The general areas of Finance are business Finance, personal Finance, and public Finance. Finance includes saving money and often includes lending money.
Limits to arbitrage	Limits to arbitrage is a theory which assumes that restrictions placed upon funds, that would ordinarily be used by rational traders to arbitrage away pricing inefficiencies, leave prices in a non-equilibrium state for protracted periods of time.
	The efficient market hypothesis assumes that whenever mispricing of a publicly-traded stock occurs as a result of an over-reaction to news, or some similar event, an opportuntity for low-risk profit is created for rational traders. The low-risk profit opportunity exists through the tool of arbitrage, which, briefly, is buying and selling differently priced items of the same value, and pocketing the difference.
Bank	A Bank is a financial institution licensed by a government. Its primary activities include borrowing and lending money. Many other financial activities were allowed over time.
Bank of New York	The Bank of New York, abbreviated BoNY or BNY, was a global financial services company that existed until its merger with the Mellon Financial Corporation on July 2, 2007. The bank now continues under the new name of The Bank of New York Mellon.
	The Bank of New York was founded on June 9, 1784, making it the oldest bank in the United States. Alexander Hamilton wrote the new bank"s constitution, and became the individual most actively involved in the organization of The Bank of New York, guiding it through its early stages.
Federal Reserve Banks	The United States Federal Reserve System consists of twelve Federal Reserve Banks, each responsible for a particular district, and some with branches.
	The twelve regional Federal Reserve Banks were established by the United States Congress as the operating arms of the nation"s central banking system. These banks were the idea of Alexander Hamilton, the first Secretary of Treasury, who started a movement advocating the creation of a central bank.
Federal Reserve Bank of New York	The Federal Reserve Bank of New York is one of the 12 Federal Reserve Banks of the United States. It is located at 33 Liberty Street, New York, NY. It is responsible for the Second District of the Federal Reserve System, which encompasses New York state, the 12 northern counties of New Jersey, Fairfield County in Connecticut, Puerto Rico, and the U. S. Virgin Islands.
	Since the founding of the Federal Reserve banking system, the Federal Reserve Bank of New York in Manhattan"s Financial District has been the place where monetary policy in the United States is implemented, although policy is decided in Washington, D.C. by the Board of Governors of the Federal Reserve System.

Chapter 12. Efficient Markets and Behavioral Finance

Chapter 12. Efficient Markets and Behavioral Finance

Hedge	A Hedge or Hedgerow is a line of closely spaced shrubs and tree species, planted and trained in such a way as to form a barrier or to mark the boundary of an area. Hedges used to separate a road from adjoining fields or one field from another, and of sufficient age to incorporate larger trees, are known as Hedgerows. It is also a simple form of topiary.
Hedge fund	A Hedge fund is an investment fund open to a limited range of investors that is permitted by regulators to undertake a wider range of investment and trading activities than other investment funds, and that, in general, pays a performance fee to its investment manager. Every Hedge fund has its own investment strategy that determines the type of investments and the methods of investment it undertakes. Hedge funds, as a class, invest in a broad range of investments including shares, debt and commodities.
Prospect theory	Prospect theory is a theory that describes decisions between alternatives that involve risk, i.e. alternatives with uncertain outcomes, where the probabilities are known. The model is descriptive: it tries to model real-life choices, rather than optimal decisions.
	Prospect theory was developed by Daniel Kahneman, professor at Princeton University"s Department of Psychology, and Amos Tversky in 1979 as a psychologically realistic alternative to expected utility theory.
Conservatism	In business, investment, and accounting, the principle or convention of conservatism has at least two meanings.
	In investment and finance, it is a strategy which aims at long-term capital appreciation with low risk. It can be characterized as moderate or cautious and is the opposite of aggressive behavior.
Portfolio theory	Modern portfolio theory (MPT) is a theory of investment which attempts to explain how investors can maximize return and minimize risk. Although MPT is widely used in practice in the financial industry and several of its creators won a Nobel prize for the theory, in recent years the basic assumptions of MPT have been widely challenged by fields such as behavioral economics, and many companies using variants of MPT have gone bankrupt in various financial crises.
	MPT is a mathematical formulation of the concept of diversification in investing, with the aim of selecting a collection of investment assets that has collectively lower risk than any individual asset.
Bias	Bias is a term used to describe a tendency or preference towards a particular perspective, ideology or result, especially when the tendency interferes with the ability to be impartial, unprejudiced, or objective.. In other words, Bias is generally seen as "one-sided". The term Biased is used to describe an action, judgment, or other outcome influenced by a prejudged perspective.
Covariance	In probability theory and statistics, Covariance is a measure of how much two variables change together. (Variance is a special case of the Covariance when the two variables are identical).
	If two variables tend to vary together (that is, when one of them is above its expected value, then the other variable tends to be above its expected value too), then the Covariance between the two variables will be positive.
Elasticity	In economics, elasticity is the ratio of the percent change in one variable to the percent change in another variable. It is a tool for measuring the responsiveness of a function to changes in parameters in a relative way. Commonly analyzed are elasticity of substitution, price and wealth.

Chapter 12. Efficient Markets and Behavioral Finance

Chapter 12. Efficient Markets and Behavioral Finance

FIFO	FIFO is an acronym for First In, First Out, an abstraction in ways of organizing and manipulation of data relative to time and prioritization. This expression describes the principle of a queue processing technique or servicing conflicting demands by ordering process by first-come, first-served (FCFS) behaviour: what comes in first is handled first, what comes in next waits until the first is finished, etc. Thus it is analogous to the behaviour of persons queueing (or "standing in line", in common American parlance), where the persons leave the queue in the order they arrive, or waiting one"s turn at a traffic control signal.
Inventory	inventory is a list for goods and materials, held available in stock by a business. It is also used for a list of the contents of a household and for a list for testamentary purposes of the possessions of someone who has died. In accounting inventory is considered an asset.
Inventory valuation	An Inventory valuation allows a company to provide a monetary value for items that make up their inventory. Inventories are usually the largest current asset of a business, and proper measurement of them is necessary to assure accurate financial statements. If inventory is not properly measured, expenses and revenues cannot be properly matched and a company could make poor business decisions.
Procter ' Gamble	Procter is a surname, and may also refer to: · Bryan Waller Procter (pseud. Barry Cornwall), English poet · Goodwin Procter, American law firm · Procter ' Gamble, consumer products multinational "
Trust	In common law legal systems, a trust is an arrangement whereby property (including real, tangible and intangible) is managed by one person (or persons) for the benefit of another. A trust is created by a settlor (or feoffor to uses), who entrusts some or all of his property to people of his choice (the trustees or feoffee to uses). The trustees hold legal title to the trust property (corpus), but they are obliged to hold the property for the benefit of one or more individuals or organizations (the beneficiary, cestui que use, or cestui que trust), usually specified by the settlor, who hold equitable title.
Stock exchange	A Stock exchange is a corporation or mutual organization which provides "trading" facilities for stock brokers and traders, to trade stocks and other securities. Stock exchanges also provide facilities for the issue and redemption of securities as well as other financial instruments and capital events including the payment of income and dividends. The securities traded on a Stock exchange include: shares issued by companies, unit trusts, derivatives, pooled investment products and bonds.
Stock split	A Stock split or stock divide increases or decreases the number of shares in a public company. The price is adjusted such that the market capitalization of the company remains the same after the split, so that dilution does not occur. Options and warrants are included.

Chapter 12. Efficient Markets and Behavioral Finance

Chapter 13. Payout Policy

Choice

There are four types of decisions, although they can be expressed in different ways. Brian Tracy, who often uses enumerated lists in his talks, breaks them down into:

· Command decisions, which can only be made by you, as the "Commander in Chief"; or owner of a company.
· Delegated decisions, which may be made by anyone, such as the color of the bike shed, and should be delegated, as the decision must be made but the Choice is inconsequential.
· Avoided decisions, where the outcome could be so severe that the Choice should not be made, as the consequences can not be recovered from if the wrong Choice is made. This will most likely result in negative actions, such as death.
· "No-brainer" decisions, where the Choice is so obvious that only one Choice can reasonably be made.

A fifth type, however, or fourth if three and four are combined as one type, is the collaborative decision, which should be made in consultation with, and by agreement of others.

Dividend

Dividends are payments made by a corporation to its shareholder members. It is the portion of corporate profits paid out to stockholders. When a corporation earns a profit or surplus, that money can be put to two uses: it can either be re-invested in the business (called retained earnings), or it can be paid to the shareholders as a Dividend.

Special dividend

A Special dividend is a payment made by a company to its shareholders that is separate from the typical recurring dividend cycle, if any, for the company. The difference may be the result of the date of issue, the amount, the type of payment, or a combination of these factors.

The amount of the dividend is declared special or significant in relation to the stock price.

Macro derivative

A macro derivative or an economic derivative is a derivative that is based on a macroeconomic figure, such as consumer confidence, jobless claims, in 2002 Goldman Sachs and Deutsche Bank announced to offer their clients auctions for derivatives based on macroeconomic key figures. In 2005 Deutsche Bank left the joint project.

Business valuation

Business valuation is a process and a set of procedures used to estimate the economic value of an owner"s interest in a business. Valuation is used by financial market participants to determine the price they are willing to pay or receive to consummate a sale of a business. In addition to estimating the selling price of a business, the same valuation tools are often used by business appraisers to resolve disputes related to estate and gift taxation, divorce litigation, allocate business purchase price among business assets, establish a formula for estimating the value of partners" ownership interest for buy-sell agreements, and many other business and legal purposes.

Dutch auction

A Dutch auction is a type of auction where the auctioneer begins with a high asking price which is lowered until some participant is willing to accept the auctioneer"s price) is reached. The winning participant pays the last announced price. This is also known as a "clock auction" or an open-outcry descending-price auction.

Greenmail

Greenmail or Greenmailing is the practice of purchasing enough shares in a firm to threaten a takeover and thereby forcing the target firm to buy those shares back at a premium in order to suspend the takeover.

The term is a neologism derived from blackmail and greenback as commentators and journalists saw the practice of said corporate raiders as attempts by well-financed individuals to blackmail a company into handing over money by using the threat of a takeover.

Corporate raids aim to generate large amounts of money by hostile takeovers of large, often undervalued or inefficient companies, by either asset stripping and/or replacing management and employees.

Chapter 13. Payout Policy

Correlation swap

A Correlation swap is an over-the-counter financial derivative that allows one to speculate on or hedge risks associated with the observed average correlation, of a collection of underlying products, where each product has periodically observable prices, as with a commodity, exchange rate, interest rate, while the floating leg pays the annualized realized correlation $\rho_{realized}$. The contract value at expiration from the pay-fixed perspective is therefore

$N_{corr}(\rho_{realized} - \rho_{strike})$

Given a set of nonnegative weights w_i on n securities, with observed pairwise correlations measured to be $\rho_{i,j}$ the weighted average correlation is defined as

$$\rho_{realized} = \frac{\sum_{i,j} w_i w_j \rho_{i,j}}{\sum_{i,j} w_i w_j}$$

No industry-standard models yet exist that have stochastic correlation and are arbitrage-free.

Tender offer

Tender offer is a corporate finance term denoting a type of takeover bid. The Tender offer is a public, open offer or invitation (usually announced in a newspaper advertisement) by a prospective acquirer to all stockholders of a publicly traded corporation (the target corporation) to tender their stock for sale at a specified price during a specified time, subject to the tendering of a minimum and maximum number of shares. In a Tender offer, the bidder contacts shareholders directly; the directors of the company may or may not have endorsed the Tender offer proposal.

Share repurchase

In some countries, including the United States and the United Kingdom, corporations can buy back their own stock in a Share repurchase from $5b in 1980 to $349b in 2005. A Share repurchase distributes cash to existing shareholders in exchange for a fraction of the firm''s outstanding equity. That is, cash is exchanged for a reduction in the number of shares outstanding.

Finance

Finance is the science of funds management. The general areas of Finance are business Finance, personal Finance, and public Finance. Finance includes saving money and often includes lending money.

Information content

In information theory (elaborated by Claude E. Shannon, 1948), self-information is a measure of the information content associated with the outcome of a random variable. It is expressed in a unit of information, for example bits, nats, or hartleys, depending on the base of the logarithm used in its calculation. The term self-information is also sometimes used as a synonym of entropy, i.e. the expected value of self-information in the first sense, because I(X;X) = H(X), where I(X;X) is the mutual information of X with itself.

Capital gains tax

A Capital gains tax is a tax charged on capital gains, the profit realized on the sale of a non-inventory asset that was purchased at a lower price. The most common capital gains are realized from the sale of stocks, bonds, precious metals and property. Not all countries implement a Capital gains tax and most have different rates of taxation for individuals and corporations.

Forward price

The Forward price (or) is the agreed upon price of an asset in a forward contract. Using the rational pricing assumption, we can express the Forward price in terms of the spot price and any dividends etc., so that there is no possibility for arbitrage.

The Forward price is given by:

$$F = S_0 e^{(r+q)T} - \sum_{i=1}^{N} D_i e^{r(T-t_i)}$$

Chapter 13. Payout Policy

Chapter 13. Payout Policy

where
F is the Forward price to be paid at time T
e^x is the exponential function
r is the risk-free interest rate
q is the cost-of-carry
S_0 is the spot price of the asset
D_i is a dividend which is guaranteed to be paid at time t_i where $0 < t_i < T$.

The two questions here are what price the short position (the seller of the asset) should offer to maximize his gain, and what price the long position (the buyer of the asset) should accept to maximize his gain?
At the very least we know that both do not want to lose any money in the deal.

Functional classification	The functional classification of a road is the class, of roads that the road belongs to. There are three main functional classes as defined by the United States Federal Highway Administration: arterial, collector, and local.
	Arterial roads generally provide the fastest method of travel and typically have low accessibility from neighboring roads.
Tax	For similar words, see Taxi
	To Tax is to impose a financial charge or other levy upon a Taxpayer (an individual or legal entity) by a state or the functional equivalent of a state such that failure to pay is punishable by law.
	Taxes are also imposed by many subnational entities. Taxes consist of direct Tax or indirect Tax, and may be paid in money or as its labour equivalent (often but not always unpaid).
Rate of return	Yield is the compound Rate of return that includes the effect of reinvesting interest or dividends.
	To the right is an example of a stock investment of one share purchased at the beginning of the year for $100.
	· The quarterly dividend is reinvested at the quarter-end stock price.
	· The number of shares purchased each quarter = ($ Dividend)/($ Stock Price).
	· The final investment value of $103.02 is a 3.02% Yield on the initial investment of $100. This is the compound yield, and this return can be considered to be the return on the investment of $100.
	To calculate the Rate of return, the investor includes the reinvested dividends in the total investment. The investor received a total of $4.06 in dividends over the year, all of which were reinvested, so the investment amount increased by $4.06.
	· Total Investment = Cost Basis = $100 + $4.06 = $104.06.
	· Capital gain/loss = $103.02 - $104.06 = -$1.04 (a capital loss)
	· ($4.06 dividends - $1.04 capital loss) / $104.06 total investment = 2.9% ROI
	The disadvantage of this ROI calculation is that it does not take into account the fact that not all the money was invested during the entire year (the dividend reinvestments occurred throughout the year).
Efficient-market hypothesis	In finance, the Efficient-market hypothesis (EMH) asserts that financial markets are "informationally efficient", stocks, bonds, or property) already reflect all known information, and instantly change to reflect new information. Therefore, according to theory, it is impossible to consistently outperform the market by using any information that the market already knows, except through luck. Information or news in the EMH is defined as anything that may affect prices that is unknowable in the present and thus appears randomly in the future.

Chapter 13. Payout Policy

Internality

An internality is a term used in behavioral economics to describe those types of behaviors that impose costs on a person in the long-run that are not taken into account when making decisions in the present. Classical Economics discourages government from creating legislation that targets internalities, because it is assumed that the consumer takes these personal costs into account when paying for the good that causes the internality. For example, cigarettes should be taxed because of the negative consumption externalities that they impose, such as second-hand smoke, not because the smoker harms him or herself by smoking.

Internal rate of return

The internal rate of return (IRR) is a rate of return used in capital budgeting to measure and compare the profitability of investments. It is also called the discounted cash flow rate of return (DCFROR) or simply the rate of return (ROR). In the context of savings and loans the IRR is also called the effective interest rate.

Dividend payout ratio

Dividend payout ratio is the fraction of net income a firm pays to its stockholders in dividends:

$$\text{Dividend payout ratio} = \frac{\text{Dividends}}{\text{Net Income for the same period}}$$

The part of the earnings not paid to investors is left for investment to provide for future earnings growth. Investors seeking high current income and limited capital growth prefer companies with high Dividend payout ratio. However investors seeking capital growth may prefer lower payout ratio because capital gains are taxed at a lower rate.

Payout ratio

Dividend payout ratio is the fraction of net income a firm pays to its stockholders in dividends:

$$\text{Dividend payout ratio} = \frac{\text{Dividends}}{\text{Net Income for the same period}}$$

The part of the earnings not paid to investors is left for investment to provide for future earnings growth. Investors seeking high current income and limited capital growth prefer companies with high Dividend payout ratio. However investors seeking capital growth may prefer lower payout ratio because capital gains are taxed at a lower rate.

Capital budgeting

Capital budgeting (or investment appraisal) is the planning process used to determine whether a firm"s long term investments such as new machinery, replacement machinery, new plants, new products, and research development projects are worth pursuing. It is budget for major capital, or investment, expenditures.

Many formal methods are used in Capital budgeting, including the techniques such as

· Accounting rate of return
· Net present value
· Profitability index
· Internal rate of return
· Modified Internal Rate of Return
· Equivalent annuity

These methods use the incremental cash flows from each potential investment, or project Techniques based on accounting earnings and accounting rules are sometimes used - though economists consider this to be improper - such as the accounting rate of return, and "return on investment." Simplified and hybrid methods are used as well, such as payback period and discounted payback period.

Each potential project"s value should be estimated using a discounted cash flow (DCF) valuation, to find its net present value (NPV).

Chapter 13. Payout Policy

Chapter 13. Payout Policy

Incentive	In economics and sociology, an incentive is any factor (financial or non-financial) that enables or motivates a particular course of action, the study of incentive structures is central to the study of all economic activity (both in terms of individual decision-making and in terms of co-operation and competition within a larger institutional structure).
Monte Carlo methods	Monte Carlo methods are a class of computational algorithms that rely on repeated random sampling to compute their results. Monte Carlo methods are often used when simulating physical and mathematical systems. Because of their reliance on repeated computation of random or pseudo-random numbers, Monte Carlo methods are most suited to calculation by a computer.
Financial distress	Financial distress is a term in Corporate Finance used to indicate a condition when promises to creditors of a company are broken or honored with difficulty. Sometimes Financial distress can lead to bankruptcy. Financial distress is usually associated with some costs to the company; these are known as costs of Financial distress.
Institutional investors	Institutional investors are organizations which pool large sums of money and invest those sums in companies. They include banks, insurance companies, retirement or pension funds, hedge funds and mutual funds. Their role in the economy is to act as highly specialized investors on behalf of others.

Chapter 14. Does Debt Policy Matter?

Capital structure	In finance, Capital structure refers to the way a corporation finances its assets through some combination of equity, debt, a firm that sells $20 billion in equity and $80 billion in debt is said to be 20% equity-financed and 80% debt-financed.
Debt	Debt is that which is owed; usually referencing assets owed, but the term can also cover moral obligations and other interactions not requiring money. In the case of assets, Debt is a means of using future purchasing power in the present before a summation has been earned. Some companies and corporations use Debt as a part of their overall corporate finance strategy.
Efficient-market hypothesis	In finance, the Efficient-market hypothesis (EMH) asserts that financial markets are "informationally efficient", stocks, bonds, or property) already reflect all known information, and instantly change to reflect new information. Therefore, according to theory, it is impossible to consistently outperform the market by using any information that the market already knows, except through luck. Information or news in the EMH is defined as anything that may affect prices that is unknowable in the present and thus appears randomly in the future.
Restructuring	restructuring is the corporate management term for the act of reorganizing the legal, ownership, operational, or better organized for its present needs. Alternate reasons f include a change of ownership or ownership structure, demerger, or a response to a crisis or major change in the business such as bankruptcy, repositioning, or buyout. restructuring may also be described as corporate restructuring, debt restructuring and financial restructuring.
Internality	An internality is a term used in behavioral economics to describe those types of behaviors that impose costs on a person in the long-run that are not taken into account when making decisions in the present. Classical Economics discourages government from creating legislation that targets internalities, because it is assumed that the consumer takes these personal costs into account when paying for the good that causes the internality. For example, cigarettes should be taxed because of the negative consumption externalities that they impose, such as second-hand smoke, not because the smoker harms him or herself by smoking.
Internal rate of return	The internal rate of return (IRR) is a rate of return used in capital budgeting to measure and compare the profitability of investments. It is also called the discounted cash flow rate of return (DCFROR) or simply the rate of return (ROR). In the context of savings and loans the IRR is also called the effective interest rate.
Leverage	In finance, leverage or leveraging refers to the use of debt to supplement investment. Companies usually leverage to increase returns to stock, as this practice can maximize gains (and losses). The easy but high-risk increases in stock prices due to leveraging at US banks has been blamed for the unusually high rate of pay for top executives during the recent banking crisis, since gains in stock are often rewarded regardless of method.
Exact laws	One particularly important physical result concerning conservation laws is Noether"s Theorem, which states that there is a one-to-one correspondence between conservation laws and differentiable symmetries of physical systems. For example, the conservation of energy follows from the time-invariance of physical systems, and the fact that physical systems behave the same regardless of how they are oriented in space gives rise to the conservation of angular momentum. A partial listing of conservation laws that are said to be exact laws, or more precisely have never been shown to be violated:

Chapter 14. Does Debt Policy Matter?

Chapter 14. Does Debt Policy Matter?

- Conservation of energy
- Conservation of linear momentum
- Conservation of angular momentum
- Conservation of electric charge
- Conservation of color charge
- Conservation of weak isospin
- Conservation of probability

There are also approximate conservation laws. These are approximately true in particular situations, such as low speeds, short time scales, or certain interactions.

- Conservation of mass (applies for low speeds)
- Conservation of baryon number .

Rate of return

Yield is the compound Rate of return that includes the effect of reinvesting interest or dividends.

To the right is an example of a stock investment of one share purchased at the beginning of the year for $100.

- The quarterly dividend is reinvested at the quarter-end stock price.
- The number of shares purchased each quarter = ($ Dividend)/($ Stock Price).
- The final investment value of $103.02 is a 3.02% Yield on the initial investment of $100. This is the compound yield, and this return can be considered to be the return on the investment of $100.

To calculate the Rate of return, the investor includes the reinvested dividends in the total investment. The investor received a total of $4.06 in dividends over the year, all of which were reinvested, so the investment amount increased by $4.06.

- Total Investment = Cost Basis = $100 + $4.06 = $104.06.
- Capital gain/loss = $103.02 - $104.06 = -$1.04 (a capital loss)
- ($4.06 dividends - $1.04 capital loss) / $104.06 total investment = 2.9% ROI

The disadvantage of this ROI calculation is that it does not take into account the fact that not all the money was invested during the entire year (the dividend reinvestments occurred throughout the year).

Risk-return spectrum

The risk-return spectrum is the relationship between the amount of return gained on an investment and the amount of risk undertaken in that investment. The more return sought, the more risk that must be undertaken.

There are various classes of possible investments, each with their own positions on the overall risk-return spectrum.

Equity

Equity, in finance and accounting, refers to the residual claim or interest of the most junior class of investors in an asset, after all liabilities are paid. If valuations placed on assets do not exceed liabilities, negative Equity exists. In an accounting context, Shareholders" Equity (or stockholders" Equity, shareholders" funds, shareholders" capital or similar terms) represents the remaining interest in assets of a company, spread among individual shareholders of common or preferred stock.

Chapter 14. Does Debt Policy Matter?

Chapter 14. Does Debt Policy Matter?

Ratio	A ratio is an expression that compares quantities relative to each other. The most common examples involve two quantities, but any number of quantities can be compared. ratios are represented mathematically by separating each quantity with a colon - for example, the ratio 2:3, which is read as the ratio "two to three".
Financial risk	Financial risk is normally any risk associated with any form of financing. Risk is probability of unfavorable condition; in financial sector it is the probability of actual return being less than expected return. There will be uncertainty in every business; the level of uncertainty present is called risk.
Return	Returns .
Securities	A security is a fungible, negotiable instrument representing financial value. Securities are broadly categorized into debt Securities (such as banknotes, bonds and debentures); equity Securities, e.g., common stocks; and derivative contracts, such as forwards, futures, options and swaps. The company or other entity issuing the security is called the issuer.
Mutual fund	A Mutual fund is a professionally managed type of collective investment scheme that pools money from many investors and invests it in stocks, bonds, short-term money market instruments, and/or other securities. The Mutual fund will have a fund manager that trades the pooled money on a regular basis. The net proceeds or losses are then typically distributed to the investors annually.
Yield curve	In finance, the yield curve is the relation between the interest rate (or cost of borrowing) and the time to maturity of the debt for a given borrower in a given currency. For example, the U.S. dollar interest rates paid on U.S. Treasury securities for various maturities are closely watched by many traders, and are commonly plotted on a graph such as the one on the right which is informally called "the yield curve." More formal mathematical descriptions of this relation are often called the term structure of interest rates.
	The yield of a debt instrument is the overall rate of return available on the investment.
Bank	A Bank is a financial institution licensed by a government. Its primary activities include borrowing and lending money. Many other financial activities were allowed over time.
Interest	In the Renaissance era, greater mobility of people facilitated an increase in commerce and the appearance of appropriate conditions for entrepreneurs to start new, lucrative businesses. Given that borrowed money was no longer strictly for consumption but for production as well, Interest was no longer viewed in the same manner. The School of Salamanca elaborated on various reasons that justified the charging of Interest: the person who received a loan benefited, and one could consider Interest as a premium paid for the risk taken by the loaning party.
Interest rates	An interest rate is the price a borrower pays for the use of money they do not own, for instance a small company might borrow from a bank to kick start their business, and the return a lender receives for deferring the use of funds, by lending it to the borrower. Interest rates are normally expressed as a percentage rate over the period of one year.
	Interest rates targets are also a vital tool of monetary policy and are used to control variables like investment, inflation, and unemployment.
Loan	A Loan is a type of debt. Like all debt instruments, a Loan entails the redistribution of financial assets over time, between the lender and the borrower.

Chapter 14. Does Debt Policy Matter?

Chapter 14. Does Debt Policy Matter?

	In a Loan, the borrower initially receives or borrows an amount of money, called the principal, from the lender, and is obligated to pay back or repay an equal amount of money to the lender at a later time.
Tax	For similar words, see Taxi
	To Tax is to impose a financial charge or other levy upon a Taxpayer (an individual or legal entity) by a state or the functional equivalent of a state such that failure to pay is punishable by law. Taxes are also imposed by many subnational entities. Taxes consist of direct Tax or indirect Tax, and may be paid in money or as its labour equivalent (often but not always unpaid).
Cost	In business, retail, and accounting, a cost is the value of money that has been used up to produce something, and hence is not available for use anymore. In economics, a cost is an alternative that is given up as a result of a decision. In business, the cost may be one of acquisition, in which case the amount of money expended to acquire it is counted as cost.
Cost of capital	In business and finance, the cost of capital is the cost of obtaining funds for, or, conversely, the required return necessary to meet its cost of financing a capital budgeting project. Said another way, it is "the minimum return that a company should make on its own investments, to earn the cash flow out of which investors can be paid their return." cost of capital encompasses the two fundamental sources of financing: the cost of debt (including bonds and loans) and the cost of equity.
	Capital (money) used for funding a business should earn returns for the capital providers who risk their capital.

Chapter 15. How Much Should a Firm Borrow?

Interest	In the Renaissance era, greater mobility of people facilitated an increase in commerce and the appearance of appropriate conditions for entrepreneurs to start new, lucrative businesses. Given that borrowed money was no longer strictly for consumption but for production as well, Interest was no longer viewed in the same manner. The School of Salamanca elaborated on various reasons that justified the charging of Interest: the person who received a loan benefited, and one could consider Interest as a premium paid for the risk taken by the loaning party.
Tax	For similar words, see Taxi To Tax is to impose a financial charge or other levy upon a Taxpayer (an individual or legal entity) by a state or the functional equivalent of a state such that failure to pay is punishable by law. Taxes are also imposed by many subnational entities. Taxes consist of direct Tax or indirect Tax, and may be paid in money or as its labour equivalent (often but not always unpaid).
Tax shield	A Tax shield is the reduction in income taxes that results from taking an allowable deduction from taxable income. For example, because interest on debt is a tax-deductible expense, taking on debt creates a Tax shield. Since a Tax shield is a way to save cash flows, it increases the value of the business, and it is an important aspect of business valuation.
Capital structure	In finance, Capital structure refers to the way a corporation finances its assets through some combination of equity, debt, a firm that sells $20 billion in equity and $80 billion in debt is said to be 20% equity-financed and 80% debt-financed.
Depreciation	Composite life equals the total Depreciable Cost divided by the total depreciation Per Year. $5,900 / $1,300 = 4.5 years. Composite depreciation Rate equals depreciation Per Year divided by total Historical Cost.
Equity	Equity, in finance and accounting, refers to the residual claim or interest of the most junior class of investors in an asset, after all liabilities are paid. If valuations placed on assets do not exceed liabilities, negative Equity exists. In an accounting context, Shareholders" Equity (or stockholders" Equity, shareholders" funds, shareholders" capital or similar terms) represents the remaining interest in assets of a company, spread among individual shareholders of common or preferred stock.
Internality	An internality is a term used in behavioral economics to describe those types of behaviors that impose costs on a person in the long-run that are not taken into account when making decisions in the present. Classical Economics discourages government from creating legislation that targets internalities, because it is assumed that the consumer takes these personal costs into account when paying for the good that causes the internality. For example, cigarettes should be taxed because of the negative consumption externalities that they impose, such as second-hand smoke, not because the smoker harms him or herself by smoking.
Internal rate of return	The internal rate of return (IRR) is a rate of return used in capital budgeting to measure and compare the profitability of investments. It is also called the discounted cash flow rate of return (DCFROR) or simply the rate of return (ROR). In the context of savings and loans the IRR is also called the effective interest rate.
Debt	Debt is that which is owed; usually referencing assets owed, but the term can also cover moral obligations and other interactions not requiring money. In the case of assets, Debt is a means of using future purchasing power in the present before a summation has been earned. Some companies and corporations use Debt as a part of their overall corporate finance strategy.

Chapter 15. How Much Should a Firm Borrow?

Chapter 15. How Much Should a Firm Borrow?

Leverage	In finance, leverage or leveraging refers to the use of debt to supplement investment. Companies usually leverage to increase returns to stock, as this practice can maximize gains (and losses). The easy but high-risk increases in stock prices due to leveraging at US banks has been blamed for the unusually high rate of pay for top executives during the recent banking crisis, since gains in stock are often rewarded regardless of method.
Financial distress	Financial distress is a term in Corporate Finance used to indicate a condition when promises to creditors of a company are broken or honored with difficulty. Sometimes Financial distress can lead to bankruptcy. Financial distress is usually associated with some costs to the company; these are known as costs of Financial distress.
Bankruptcy	bankruptcy is a legally declared inability or impairment of ability of an individual or organization to pay its creditors. Creditors may file a bankruptcy petition against a debtor ("involuntary bankruptcy") in an effort to recoup a portion of what they are owed or initiate a restructuring. In the majority of cases, however, bankruptcy is initiated by the debtor (a "voluntary bankruptcy" that is filed by the insolvent individual or organization).
Cost	In business, retail, and accounting, a cost is the value of money that has been used up to produce something, and hence is not available for use anymore. In economics, a cost is an alternative that is given up as a result of a decision. In business, the cost may be one of acquisition, in which case the amount of money expended to acquire it is counted as cost.
Bankruptcy costs	Within the theory of corporate finance, Bankruptcy costs of debt are the increased costs of financing with debt instead of equity that result from a higher probability of bankruptcy. The fact that bankruptcy is generally a costly process in itself and not only a transfer of ownership implies that these costs negatively affect the total value of the firm. These costs can be thought of as a financial cost, in the sense that the cost of financing increases because the probability of bankruptcy increases.
Restructuring	restructuring is the corporate management term for the act of reorganizing the legal, ownership, operational, or better organized for its present needs. Alternate reasons f include a change of ownership or ownership structure, demerger, or a response to a crisis or major change in the business such as bankruptcy, repositioning, or buyout. restructuring may also be described as corporate restructuring, debt restructuring and financial restructuring.
Trade-off	A trade-off (or tradeoff) is a situation that involves losing one quality or aspect of something in return for gaining another quality or aspect. It implies a decision to be made with full comprehension of both the upside and downside of a particular choice. In economics the term is expressed as opportunity cost, referring to the most preferred alternative given up.
Trade-off theory	The trade-off theory of Capital Structure refers to the idea that a company chooses how much debt finance and how much equity finance to use by balancing the costs and benefits. The classical version of the hypothesis goes back to Kraus and Litzenberger who considered a balance between the dead-weight costs of bankruptcy and the tax saving benefits of debt. Often agency costs are also included in the balance.

Chapter 15. How Much Should a Firm Borrow?

Chapter 15. How Much Should a Firm Borrow?

Trade-off theory of capital structure	The Trade-Off Theory of Capital Structure refers to the idea that a company chooses how much debt finance and how much equity finance to use by balancing the costs and benefits. The classical version of the hypothesis goes back to Kraus and Litzenberger who considered a balance between the dead-weight costs of bankruptcy and the tax saving benefits of debt. Often agency costs are also included in the balance.
Incentive	In economics and sociology, an incentive is any factor (financial or non-financial) that enables or motivates a particular course of action, the study of incentive structures is central to the study of all economic activity (both in terms of individual decision-making and in terms of co-operation and competition within a larger institutional structure).
Correlation swap	A Correlation swap is an over-the-counter financial derivative that allows one to speculate on or hedge risks associated with the observed average correlation, of a collection of underlying products, where each product has periodically observable prices, as with a commodity, exchange rate, interest rate, while the floating leg pays the annualized realized correlation $\rho_{realized}$. The contract value at expiration from the pay-fixed perspective is therefore $N_{corr}(\rho_{realized} - \rho_{strike})$ Given a set of nonnegative weights w_i on n securities, with observed pairwise correlations measured to be $\rho_{i,j}$ the weighted average correlation is defined as $$\rho_{realized} = \frac{\sum_{i,j} w_i w_j \rho_{i,j}}{\sum_{i,j} w_i w_j}$$ No industry-standard models yet exist that have stochastic correlation and are arbitrage-free.
Common stock	Common stock is a form of corporate equity ownership, a type of security. It is called "common" to distinguish it from preferred stock. In the event of bankruptcy, Common stock investors receive their funds after preferred stock holders, bondholders, creditors, etc.
Valuation	In finance, valuation is the process of estimating the potential market value of a financial asset or liability. valuations can be done on assets (for example, investments in marketable securities such as stocks, options, business enterprises, or intangible assets such as patents and trademarks) or on liabilities (e.g., Bonds issued by a company). valuations are required in many contexts including investment analysis, capital budgeting, merger and acquisition transactions, financial reporting, taxable events to determine the proper tax liability, and in litigation. valuation of financial assets is done using one or more of these types of models: · Discounted Cash Flows determine the value by estimating the expected future earnings from owning the asset discounted to their present value. · Relative value models determine the value based on the market prices of similar assets. · Option pricing models are used for certain types of financial assets (e.g., warrants, put options, call options, employee stock options, investments with embedded options such as a callable bond) and are a complex present value model.
Chief brand officer	A Chief brand officer is a relatively new executive level position at a corporation, company, organization, typically reporting directly to the CEO or board of directors. The Chief brand officer is responsible for a brand"s image, experience, and promise, and propagating it throughout all aspects of the company. The brand officer oversees marketing, advertising, design, public relations and customer service departments. The brand equity of a company is seen as becoming increasingly dependent on the role of a Chief brand officer.

Chapter 15. How Much Should a Firm Borrow?

Chapter 15. How Much Should a Firm Borrow?

Companies that currently employ a Chief brand officer include:

- Srinivas Kumar, Baskin-Robbins Worldwide
- Michael Keller, Dairy Queen
- Will Kussell, Dunkin" Brands, Inc.
- Trey Hall, Boston Market Corporation
- Allen Schiffenbaure, G 2 Marketing Group
- Alan Bergstrom, Storyminers Inc.
- Brian Igoe, Metabolix, Inc.
- Phil Mcaveety, Luxury Collection
- Mark I. McCallum, Brown-Forman Corporation
- Phil McAveety, Starwood Hotels ' Resorts Worldwide, Inc.
- Danny Meisenheimer, Souper Salad, Inc

Leveraged buyout	A Leveraged buyout (or LBO), or "bootstrap" transaction) occurs when a financial sponsor acquires a controlling interest in a company"s equity and where a significant percentage of the purchase price is financed through leverage (borrowing). The assets of the acquired company are used as collateral for the borrowed capital, sometimes with assets of the acquiring company. The bonds or other paper issued for Leveraged buyouts are commonly considered not to be investment grade because of the significant risks involved.
	Companies of all sizes and industries have been the target of Leveraged buyout transactions, although because of the importance of debt and the ability of the acquired firm to make regular loan payments after the completion of a Leveraged buyout, some features of potential target firms make for more attractive leverage buyout candidates, including:
	· Low existing debt loads; · A multi-year history of stable and recurring cash flows; · Hard assets (property, plant and equipment, inventory, receivables) that may be used as collateral for lower cost secured debt; · The potential for new management to make operational or other improvements to the firm to boost cash flows; · Market conditions and perceptions that depress the valuation or stock price.
Asset	In business and accounting, Assets are economic resources owned by business or company. Anything tangible or intangible that one possesses, usually considered as applicable to the payment of one"s debts is considered an Asset. Simplistically stated, Assets are things of value that can be readily converted into cash (although cash itself is also considered an Asset).
Information asymmetry	In economics and contract theory, information asymmetry deals with the study of decisions in transactions where one party has more or better information than the other. This creates an imbalance of power in transactions which can sometimes cause the transactions to go awry. Examples of this problem are adverse selection and moral hazard.

Chapter 15. How Much Should a Firm Borrow?

Chapter 15. How Much Should a Firm Borrow?

Pecking order	Pecking order or just peck order is a hierarchical system of social organization in animals. It was first described from the behaviour of poultry by Thorleif Schjelderup-Ebbe in 1921 under the German terms Hackordnung or Hackliste and introduced into English in 1925. The original usage of "peck order" referred to expression of dominance of birds. Dominance in chickens is expressed in various behaviours including pecking which was used by Schjelderup-Ebbe as a measure of dominance.
Choice	There are four types of decisions, although they can be expressed in different ways. Brian Tracy, who often uses enumerated lists in his talks, breaks them down into: · Command decisions, which can only be made by you, as the "Commander in Chief"; or owner of a company. · Delegated decisions, which may be made by anyone, such as the color of the bike shed, and should be delegated, as the decision must be made but the Choice is inconsequential. · Avoided decisions, where the outcome could be so severe that the Choice should not be made, as the consequences can not be recovered from if the wrong Choice is made. This will most likely result in negative actions, such as death. · "No-brainer" decisions, where the Choice is so obvious that only one Choice can reasonably be made. A fifth type, however, or fourth if three and four are combined as one type, is the collaborative decision, which should be made in consultation with, and by agreement of others.
Free cash flow	In corporate finance, Free cash flow is cash flow available for distribution among all the securities holders of an organization. They include equity holders, debt holders, preferred stock holders, convertible security holders, and so on. Note that the first three lines above are calculated for you on the standard Statement of Cash Flows.
Market timing	Market timing is the strategy of making buy or sell decisions of financial assets (often stocks) by attempting to predict future market price movements. The prediction may be based on an outlook of market or economic conditions resulting from technical or fundamental analysis. This is an investment strategy based on the outlook for an aggregate market, rather than for a particular financial asset.

Chapter 15. How Much Should a Firm Borrow?

Chapter 16. Financing and Valuation

Adjusted present value	Adjusted present value is a business valuation method. Adjusted present value is the net present value of a project if financed solely by ownership equity plus the present value of all the benefits of financing. It was first studied by Stewart Myers, a professor at the MIT Sloan School of Management and later theorized by Lorenzo Peccati, professor at the Bocconi University, in 1973. The method is to calculate the NPV of the project as if it is all-equity financed (so called base case).
Capital structure	In finance, Capital structure refers to the way a corporation finances its assets through some combination of equity, debt, a firm that sells $20 billion in equity and $80 billion in debt is said to be 20% equity-financed and 80% debt-financed.
Debt	Debt is that which is owed; usually referencing assets owed, but the term can also cover moral obligations and other interactions not requiring money. In the case of assets, Debt is a means of using future purchasing power in the present before a summation has been earned. Some companies and corporations use Debt as a part of their overall corporate finance strategy.
Efficient-market hypothesis	In finance, the Efficient-market hypothesis (EMH) asserts that financial markets are "informationally efficient", stocks, bonds, or property) already reflect all known information, and instantly change to reflect new information. Therefore, according to theory, it is impossible to consistently outperform the market by using any information that the market already knows, except through luck. Information or news in the EMH is defined as anything that may affect prices that is unknowable in the present and thus appears randomly in the future.
Equity	Equity, in finance and accounting, refers to the residual claim or interest of the most junior class of investors in an asset, after all liabilities are paid. If valuations placed on assets do not exceed liabilities, negative Equity exists. In an accounting context, Shareholders" Equity (or stockholders" Equity, shareholders" funds, shareholders" capital or similar terms) represents the remaining interest in assets of a company, spread among individual shareholders of common or preferred stock.
Cost	In business, retail, and accounting, a cost is the value of money that has been used up to produce something, and hence is not available for use anymore. In economics, a cost is an alternative that is given up as a result of a decision. In business, the cost may be one of acquisition, in which case the amount of money expended to acquire it is counted as cost.
Cost of capital	In business and finance, the cost of capital is the cost of obtaining funds for, or, conversely, the required return necessary to meet its cost of financing a capital budgeting project. Said another way, it is "the minimum return that a company should make on its own investments, to earn the cash flow out of which investors can be paid their return." cost of capital encompasses the two fundamental sources of financing: the cost of debt (including bonds and loans) and the cost of equity. Capital (money) used for funding a business should earn returns for the capital providers who risk their capital.
Discount rate	The Discount rate is an interest rate a central bank charges depository institutions that borrow reserves from it. The term Discount rate has two meanings: · the same as interest rate; the term "discount" does not refer to the meaning of the word, but to the purpose of using the quantity, such as computations of present value, e.g. net present value or discounted cash flow

Chapter 16. Financing and Valuation

Chapter 16. Financing and Valuation

· the annual effective Discount rate, which is the annual interest divided by the capital including that interest; this rate is lower than the interest rate; it corresponds to using the value after a year as the nominal value, and seeing the initial value as the nominal value minus a discount; it is used for Treasury Bills and similar financial instruments

The annual effective Discount rate is the annual interest divided by the capital including that interest, which is the interest rate divided by 100% plus the interest rate. It is the annual discount factor to be applied to the future cash flow, to find the discount, subtracted from a future value to find the value one year earlier.

For example, suppose there is a government bond that sells for $95 and pays $100 in a year"s time.

Macro derivative	A macro derivative or an economic derivative is a derivative that is based on a macroeconomic figure, such as consumer confidence, jobless claims, in 2002 Goldman Sachs and Deutsche Bank announced to offer their clients auctions for derivatives based on macroeconomic key figures. In 2005 Deutsche Bank left the joint project.
Business valuation	Business valuation is a process and a set of procedures used to estimate the economic value of an owner"s interest in a business. Valuation is used by financial market participants to determine the price they are willing to pay or receive to consummate a sale of a business. In addition to estimating the selling price of a business, the same valuation tools are often used by business appraisers to resolve disputes related to estate and gift taxation, divorce litigation, allocate business purchase price among business assets, establish a formula for estimating the value of partners" ownership interest for buy-sell agreements, and many other business and legal purposes.
Free cash flow	In corporate finance, Free cash flow is cash flow available for distribution among all the securities holders of an organization. They include equity holders, debt holders, preferred stock holders, convertible security holders, and so on. Note that the first three lines above are calculated for you on the standard Statement of Cash Flows.
Pecking order	Pecking order or just peck order is a hierarchical system of social organization in animals. It was first described from the behaviour of poultry by Thorleif Schjelderup-Ebbe in 1921 under the German terms Hackordnung or Hackliste and introduced into English in 1925. The original usage of "peck order" referred to expression of dominance of birds. Dominance in chickens is expressed in various behaviours including pecking which was used by Schjelderup-Ebbe as a measure of dominance.
Choice	There are four types of decisions, although they can be expressed in different ways. Brian Tracy, who often uses enumerated lists in his talks, breaks them down into: · Command decisions, which can only be made by you, as the "Commander in Chief"; or owner of a company. · Delegated decisions, which may be made by anyone, such as the color of the bike shed, and should be delegated, as the decision must be made but the Choice is inconsequential. · Avoided decisions, where the outcome could be so severe that the Choice should not be made, as the consequences can not be recovered from if the wrong Choice is made. This will most likely result in negative actions, such as death. · "No-brainer" decisions, where the Choice is so obvious that only one Choice can reasonably be made. A fifth type, however, or fourth if three and four are combined as one type, is the collaborative decision, which should be made in consultation with, and by agreement of others.

Chapter 16. Financing and Valuation

Chapter 16. Financing and Valuation

Liquidation — In law, liquidation refers to the process by which a company (or part of a company) is brought to an end, and the assets and property of the company redistributed. liquidation can also be referred to as winding-up or dissolution, although dissolution technically refers to the last stage of liquidation. The process of liquidation also arises when customs, an authority or agency in a country responsible for collecting and safeguarding customs duties, determines the final computation or ascertainment of the duties or drawback accruing on an entry.

Liquidation value — liquidation value is the likely price of an asset when it is allowed insufficient time to sell on the open market, thereby reducing its exposure to potential buyers. liquidation value is typically lower than fair market value. Unlike cash or securities, certain illiquid assets, like real estate, often require a period of several months in order to obtain their fair market value in a sale, and will generally sell for a significantly lower price if a sale is forced to occur in a shorter time period.

Current liabilities — In finance, Current liabilities are considered liabilities of the business that are to be settled in cash within the fiscal year or the operating cycle, whichever period is longer.

For example, accounts payable for goods, services or supplies that were purchased for use in the operation of the business and payable within a normal period of time would be Current liabilities.

Bonds, mortgages and loans that are payable over a term exceeding one year would be fixed liabilities or long-term liabilities.

Liabilities — In financial accounting, a liability is defined as an obligation of an entity arising from past transactions or events, the settlement of which may result in the transfer or use of assets, provision of services or other yielding of economic benefits in the future.

· All type of borrowing from persons or banks for improving a business or person income which is payable during short or long time.
· They embody a duty or responsibility to others that entails settlement by future transfer or use of assets, provision of services or other yielding of economic benefits, at a specified or determinable date, on occurrence of a specified event, or on demand;
· The duty or responsibility obligates the entity leaving it little or no discretion to avoid it; and,
· The transaction or event obligating the entity has already occurred.

liabilities in financial accounting need not be legally enforceable; but can be based on equitable obligations or constructive obligations. An equitable obligation is a duty based on ethical or moral considerations.

Short-run — In economics, the concept of the short-run refers to the decision-making time frame of a firm in which at least one factor of production is fixed. Costs which are fixed in the short-run have no impact on a firms decisions. For example a firm can raise output by increasing the amount of labour through overtime.

A generic firm can make three changes in the short-run:

· Increase production
· Decrease production
· Shut down

In the short-run, a profit maximizing firm will:

Chapter 16. Financing and Valuation

Chapter 16. Financing and Valuation

	· Increase production if marginal cost is less than price; · Decrease production if marginal cost is greater than price; · Continue producing if average variable cost is less than price, even if average total cost is greater than price; · Shut down if average variable cost is greater than price.
Bond valuation	Bond valuation is the process of determining the fair price of a bond.
	As with any security or capital investment, the fair value of a bond is the present value of the stream of cash flows it is expected to generate. Hence, the value of a bond is determined by discounting the bond"s expected cash flows to the present using the appropriate discount rate.
Michael Robert Milken	Michael Robert Milken is an American financier and philanthropist noted for his role in the development of the market for high-yield bonds during the 1970s and 1980s, for his 1990 guilty plea to multiple felony charges that he violated US securities laws, and for his funding of medical research.
	Milken was indicted on 98 counts of racketeering and securities fraud in 1989 as the result of an insider trading investigation. After a plea bargain, he pled guilty to six securities and reporting violations but was never convicted of racketeering or insider trading.
Ratio	A ratio is an expression that compares quantities relative to each other. The most common examples involve two quantities, but any number of quantities can be compared. ratios are represented mathematically by separating each quantity with a colon - for example, the ratio 2:3, which is read as the ratio "two to three".
Cost of equity	In finance, the cost of equity is the minimum rate of return a firm must offer shareholders to compensate for waiting for their returns, and for bearing some risk.
	The cost of equity capital for a particular company is the rate of return on investment that is required by the company"s ordinary shareholders. The return consists both of dividend and capital gains, e.g. increases in the share price.
Return	Returns .
Rebalancing	rebalancing is the action of bringing a portfolio of investments that has deviated away from one"s target asset allocation back into line. Under-weighted securities can be purchased with newly saved money; alternatively, over-weighted securities can be sold to purchase under-weighted securities.
	The investments in a portfolio will perform according to the market.
Internality	An internality is a term used in behavioral economics to describe those types of behaviors that impose costs on a person in the long-run that are not taken into account when making decisions in the present. Classical Economics discourages government from creating legislation that targets internalities, because it is assumed that the consumer takes these personal costs into account when paying for the good that causes the internality. For example, cigarettes should be taxed because of the negative consumption externalities that they impose, such as second-hand smoke, not because the smoker harms him or herself by smoking.

Chapter 16. Financing and Valuation

Internal rate of return	The internal rate of return (IRR) is a rate of return used in capital budgeting to measure and compare the profitability of investments. It is also called the discounted cash flow rate of return (DCFROR) or simply the rate of return (ROR). In the context of savings and loans the IRR is also called the effective interest rate.
Leverage	In finance, leverage or leveraging refers to the use of debt to supplement investment. Companies usually leverage to increase returns to stock, as this practice can maximize gains (and losses). The easy but high-risk increases in stock prices due to leveraging at US banks has been blamed for the unusually high rate of pay for top executives during the recent banking crisis, since gains in stock are often rewarded regardless of method.
Leveraged buyout	A Leveraged buyout (or LBO), or "bootstrap" transaction) occurs when a financial sponsor acquires a controlling interest in a company"s equity and where a significant percentage of the purchase price is financed through leverage (borrowing). The assets of the acquired company are used as collateral for the borrowed capital, sometimes with assets of the acquiring company. The bonds or other paper issued for Leveraged buyouts are commonly considered not to be investment grade because of the significant risks involved. Companies of all sizes and industries have been the target of Leveraged buyout transactions, although because of the importance of debt and the ability of the acquired firm to make regular loan payments after the completion of a Leveraged buyout, some features of potential target firms make for more attractive leverage buyout candidates, including: · Low existing debt loads; · A multi-year history of stable and recurring cash flows; · Hard assets (property, plant and equipment, inventory, receivables) that may be used as collateral for lower cost secured debt; · The potential for new management to make operational or other improvements to the firm to boost cash flows; · Market conditions and perceptions that depress the valuation or stock price.
Interest	In the Renaissance era, greater mobility of people facilitated an increase in commerce and the appearance of appropriate conditions for entrepreneurs to start new, lucrative businesses. Given that borrowed money was no longer strictly for consumption but for production as well, Interest was no longer viewed in the same manner. The School of Salamanca elaborated on various reasons that justified the charging of Interest: the person who received a loan benefited, and one could consider Interest as a premium paid for the risk taken by the loaning party.
Tax	For similar words, see Taxi To Tax is to impose a financial charge or other levy upon a Taxpayer (an individual or legal entity) by a state or the functional equivalent of a state such that failure to pay is punishable by law. Taxes are also imposed by many subnational entities. Taxes consist of direct Tax or indirect Tax, and may be paid in money or as its labour equivalent (often but not always unpaid).
Tax shield	A Tax shield is the reduction in income taxes that results from taking an allowable deduction from taxable income. For example, because interest on debt is a tax-deductible expense, taking on debt creates a Tax shield. Since a Tax shield is a way to save cash flows, it increases the value of the business, and it is an important aspect of business valuation.
Depreciation	Composite life equals the total Depreciable Cost divided by the total depreciation Per Year. $5,900 / $1,300 = 4.5 years.

Chapter 16. Financing and Valuation

Chapter 16. Financing and Valuation

	Composite depreciation Rate equals depreciation Per Year divided by total Historical Cost.
Government National Mortgage Association	The Government National Mortgage Association (Government National Mortgage Association,) is a U.S. government-owned corporation within the Department of Housing and Urban Development (HUD), and is headquartered in Washington, D.C.. Ginnie Mae provides guarantees on mortgage-backed securities (MBS) backed by federally insured or guaranteed loans, mainly loans issued by the Federal Housing Administration, Department of Veterans Affairs, Rural Housing Service, and Office of Public and Indian Housing. Ginnie Mae securities are the only MBS that are guaranteed by the United States government.
Black-Scholes	The term Black-Scholes refers to three closely related concepts: · The Black-Scholes model is a mathematical model of the market for an equity, in which the equity"s price is a stochastic process. · The Black-Scholes PDE is a partial differential equation which (in the model) must be satisfied by the price of a derivative on the equity. · The Black-Scholes formula is the result obtained by solving the Black-Scholes PDE for a European call option. Fischer Black and Myron Scholes first articulated the Black-Scholes formula in their 1973 paper, "The Pricing of Options and Corporate Liabilities." The foundation for their research relied on work developed by scholars such as Jack L. Treynor, Paul Samuelson, A. James Boness, Sheen T. Kassouf, and Edward O. Thorp. The fundamental insight of Black-Scholes is that the option is implicitly priced if the stock is traded.
Call option	A Call option is a financial contract between two parties, the buyer and the seller of this type of option. It is the option to buy shares of stock at a specified time in the future. Often it is simply labeled a "call".
Correlation swap	A Correlation swap is an over-the-counter financial derivative that allows one to speculate on or hedge risks associated with the observed average correlation, of a collection of underlying products, where each product has periodically observable prices, as with a commodity, exchange rate, interest rate, while the floating leg pays the annualized realized correlation $\rho_{realized}$. The contract value at expiration from the pay-fixed perspective is therefore $N_{corr}(\rho_{realized} - \rho_{strike})$ Given a set of nonnegative weights w_i on n securities, with observed pairwise correlations measured to be $\rho_{i,j}$ the weighted average correlation is defined as $$\rho_{\text{realized}} = \frac{\sum_{i,j} w_i w_j \rho_{i,j}}{\sum_{i,j} w_i w_j}$$ No industry-standard models yet exist that have stochastic correlation and are arbitrage-free.
Put option	A Put option is a financial contract between two parties, the seller (writer) and the buyer of the option. The buyer acquires a short position with the right, but not the obligation, to sell the underlying instrument at an agreed-upon price (the strike price). If the buyer exercises his right to sell the option, the seller is obliged to buy it at the strike price.

Chapter 16. Financing and Valuation

Chapter 16. Financing and Valuation

Put-call parity	In financial mathematics, Put-call parity defines a relationship between the price of a call option and a put option--both with the identical strike price and expiry. To derive the Put-call parity relationship, the assumption is that the options are not exercised before expiration day, which necessarily applies to European options. Put-call parity can be derived in a manner that is largely model independent.
Incentive	In economics and sociology, an incentive is any factor (financial or non-financial) that enables or motivates a particular course of action, the study of incentive structures is central to the study of all economic activity (both in terms of individual decision-making and in terms of co-operation and competition within a larger institutional structure).
Real option	In corporate finance, real options analysis or ROA applies put option and call option valuation techniques to capital budgeting decisions. A real option itself, is the right -- but not the obligation -- to undertake some business decision; typically the option to make, abandon, expand, or shrink a capital investment. For example, the opportunity to invest in the expansion of a firm"s factory, or alternatively to sell the factory, is a real option.
Financial distress	Financial distress is a term in Corporate Finance used to indicate a condition when promises to creditors of a company are broken or honored with difficulty. Sometimes Financial distress can lead to bankruptcy. Financial distress is usually associated with some costs to the company; these are known as costs of Financial distress.
Dividend	Dividends are payments made by a corporation to its shareholder members. It is the portion of corporate profits paid out to stockholders. When a corporation earns a profit or surplus, that money can be put to two uses: it can either be re-invested in the business (called retained earnings), or it can be paid to the shareholders as a Dividend.
Dividend payout ratio	Dividend payout ratio is the fraction of net income a firm pays to its stockholders in dividends: $$\text{Dividend payout ratio} = \frac{\text{Dividends}}{\text{Net Income for the same period}}$$ The part of the earnings not paid to investors is left for investment to provide for future earnings growth. Investors seeking high current income and limited capital growth prefer companies with high Dividend payout ratio. However investors seeking capital growth may prefer lower payout ratio because capital gains are taxed at a lower rate.
Market risk	Market risk is the risk that the value of an investment will decrease due to moves in market factors. The four standard Market risk factors are: · Equity risk, the risk that stock prices will change. · Interest rate risk, the risk that interest rates will change. · Currency risk, the risk that foreign exchange rates will change. · Commodity risk, the risk that commodity prices (e.g. corn, copper, crude oil) will change. As with other forms of risk, Market risk may be measured in a number of ways. Traditionally, this is done using a Value at Risk methodology.
Discounted cash flow	In finance, the Discounted cash flow approach describes a method of valuing a project, company, that reflects the risk of the cashflows.

Chapter 16. Financing and Valuation

Chapter 16. Financing and Valuation

Common stock	Common stock is a form of corporate equity ownership, a type of security. It is called "common" to distinguish it from preferred stock. In the event of bankruptcy, Common stock investors receive their funds after preferred stock holders, bondholders, creditors, etc.
Dot-com bubble	The "dot-com bubble" (or) was a speculative bubble covering roughly 1998-2001 (with a climax on March 10, 2000 with the NASDAQ peaking at 5132.52) during which stock markets in Western nations saw their equity value rise rapidly from growth in the more recent Internet sector and related fields. While the latter part was a boom and bust cycle, the Internet boom sometimes is meant to refer to the steady commercial growth of the Internet with the advent of the world wide web as exemplified by the first release of the Mosaic web browser in 1993 and continuing through the 1990s.
	The period was marked by the founding (and, in many cases, spectacular failure) of a group of new Internet-based companies commonly referred to as dot-coms.
Hedge	A Hedge or Hedgerow is a line of closely spaced shrubs and tree species, planted and trained in such a way as to form a barrier or to mark the boundary of an area. Hedges used to separate a road from adjoining fields or one field from another, and of sufficient age to incorporate larger trees, are known as Hedgerows. It is also a simple form of topiary.
Replicating portfolios	In the valuation of a life insurance company, the actuary considers a series of future uncertain cashflows (including incoming premiums and outgoing claims, for example) and attempts to put a value on these cashflows. There are many ways of calculating such a value , but these approaches are often arbitrary in that the interest rate chosen for discounting is itself rather arbitrarily chosen.
	One possible approach, and one that is gaining increasing attention, is the use of Replicating portfolios or hedge portfolios.
Certainty equivalent	A risk premium is the minimum difference a person requires to be willing to take an uncertain bet, between the expected value of the bet and the certain value that he is indifferent to.
	The certainty equivalent is the guaranteed payoff at which a person is "indifferent" between accepting the guaranteed payoff and a higher but uncertain payoff. (It is the amount of the higher payout minus the risk premium).
Expected utility theorem	In economics, game theory, and decision theory the expected utility theorem or expected utility hypothesis predicts that the "betting preferences" of people with regard to uncertain outcomes (gambles) can be described by a mathematical relation which takes into account the size of a payout (whether in money or other goods), the probability of occurrence, risk aversion, and the different utility of the same payout to people with different assets or personal preferences. It is a more sophisticated theory than simply predicting that choices will be made based on expected value (which takes into account only the size of the payout and the probability of occurrence).
	Daniel Bernoulli described the complete theory in 1738. John von Neumann and Oskar Morgenstern reinterpreted and presented an axiomatization of the same theory in 1944. They proved that any "normal" preference relation over a finite set of states can be written as an expected utility, sometimes referred to as von Neumann-Morgenstern utility.
Decision tree	A decision tree (or tree diagram) is a decision support tool that uses a tree-like graph or model of decisions and their possible consequences, including chance event outcomes, resource costs, and utility. decision trees are commonly used in operations research, specifically in decision analysis, to help identify a strategy most likely to reach a goal. Another use of decision trees is as a descriptive means for calculating conditional probabilities.

Chapter 16. Financing and Valuation

Chapter 16. Financing and Valuation

Outsourcing

Outsourcing is subcontracting a service such as product design or manufacturing, to a third-party company. The decision to outsource is often made in the interest of lowering cost or making better use of time and energy costs, redirecting or conserving energy directed at the competencies of a particular business, or to make more efficient use of land, labor, capital, (information) technology and resources. Outsourcing became part of the business lexicon during the 1980s.

Functional classification

The functional classification of a road is the class, of roads that the road belongs to. There are three main functional classes as defined by the United States Federal Highway Administration: arterial, collector, and local.

Arterial roads generally provide the fastest method of travel and typically have low accessibility from neighboring roads.

Securities

A security is a fungible, negotiable instrument representing financial value. Securities are broadly categorized into debt Securities (such as banknotes, bonds and debentures); equity Securities, e.g., common stocks; and derivative contracts, such as forwards, futures, options and swaps. The company or other entity issuing the security is called the issuer.

Securities and Exchange Commission

The U.S. Securities and Exchange Commission (commonly known as the SEC) is an independent agency of the United States government which holds primary responsibility for enforcing the federal securities laws and regulating the securities industry, the nation"s stock and options exchanges, and other electronic securities markets. The SEC was created by section 4 of the Securities Exchange Act of 1934 . In addition to the 1934 Act that created it, the SEC enforces the Securities Act of 1933, the Trust Indenture Act of 1939, the Investment Company Act of 1940, the Investment Advisers Act of 1940, the Sarbanes-Oxley Act of 2002 and other statutes.

- 1 Commission members
- 2 Overview
- 3 History
- 4 Chairs and commissioners
- 5 Structure
- 6 Relationship to other agencies
- 7 Related legislation
- 8 SEC communications

- 8.1 Comment letters
- 8.2 No-action letters
- 9 Regulatory action in the credit crunch
- 10 Regulatory failures
- 11

Prior to the enactment of the federal securities laws and the creation of the SEC, there existed so-called Blue Sky Laws, which were enacted and enforced at the state level.

Chapter 16. Financing and Valuation

Chapter 16. Financing and Valuation

U.S. Securities and Exchange Commission	The U.S. Securities and Exchange Commission (commonly known as the SEC) is an independent agency of the United States government which holds primary responsibility for enforcing the federal securities laws and regulating the securities industry, the nation"s stock and options exchanges, and other electronic securities markets. The SEC was created by section 4 of the Securities Exchange Act of 1934 . In addition to the 1934 Act that created it, the SEC enforces the Securities Act of 1933, the Trust Indenture Act of 1939, the Investment Company Act of 1940, the Investment Advisers Act of 1940, the Sarbanes-Oxley Act of 2002 and other statutes. · 1 Commission members · 2 Overview · 3 History · 4 Chairs and commissioners · 5 Structure · 6 Relationship to other agencies · 7 Related legislation · 8 SEC communications · 8.1 Comment letters · 8.2 No-action letters · 9 Regulatory action in the credit crunch · 10 Regulatory failures · 11 Prior to the enactment of the federal securities laws and the creation of the SEC, there existed so-called Blue Sky Laws, which were enacted and enforced at the state level.
Insurance	Insurance, in law and economics, is a form of risk management primarily used to hedge against the risk of a contingent loss. Insurance is defined as the equitable transfer of the risk of a loss, from one entity to another, in exchange for a premium, and can be thought of as a guaranteed and known small loss to prevent a large, possibly devastating loss. An insurer is a company selling the Insurance; an insured or policyholder is the person or entity buying the Insurance.
Portfolio insurance	Portfolio insurance is a method of hedging a portfolio of stocks against the market risk by short selling stock index futures. This hedging technique is frequently used by institutional investors when the market direction is uncertain or volatile. Short selling index futures can offset any downturns, but it also hinders any gains.
Risk management	Risk Management is a research programme set up by the Geneva Association the engineering and academic communities and policy makers to discuss risk issues; promoting the concept of the insurability of risks as the natural borderline between State legislation and the market economy; identifying new opportunities for insurers in the emerging sustainability concept in order to enlarge the field of insurable risks. · What are the vulnerabilities in our industrial and services value-added processes? · Where are the mechanisms for understanding, managing and mitigating these risks? · How can insurance cope with a more complex and demanding risk scenario? · What is the new risk environment that has been created in recent years? · What about technologies being a new source of vulnerability?

Chapter 16. Financing and Valuation

Chapter 16. Financing and Valuation

Risk Management Etudes et Dossiers, Working Paper Series, The Geneva Association

The Geneva Risk and Insurance Review Pensions and Life Insurance and Risk Management/M.O.R.E, The Geneva Papers on Risk and Insurance - Issues and Practice, Vol.29 - No.3 / July 2004, Palgrave Macmillan

Special Issue on Risk Management Strategic Issues in Risk Management and Insurance, The Geneva Papers on Risk and Insurance - Issues and Practice, Vol.24 - No.3 / July 1999, Palgrave Macmillan

Issues in Risk Management and Insurance Risk Management Strategies, The Geneva Papers on Risk and Insurance - Issues and Practice, No.80 / July 1996

Risk Management Issues 1973-1993 Twenty Years of Initiatives and Research on the Economic Role of Insurance and Risk Management in Modern Society, The Geneva Papers on Risk and Insurance - Issues and Practice, No.68 / July 1993

Risk Management Studies Hazardous Waste Management, The Geneva Papers on Risk and Insurance - Issues and Practice, No.51 / April 1989

Risk and Society Risk and Insurance Issues, The Geneva Papers on Risk and Insurance - Issues and Practice, No.44 / July 1987

· The Geneva Association website (known as the International Association for the Study of Insurance Economics)

· The GA M.O.R.E Programme web page, Management of Risk in Engineering

· The Risk Institute website

· The ARIA website, the American Risk and Insurance Association

Variance — In probability theory and statistics, the Variance of a random variable or distribution is the expected square deviation of that variable from its expected value or mean). For example, a perfect die, when thrown, has expected value 7/2, expected deviation 3/2 (the mean of the equally likely absolute deviations 1/2, 3/2, 5/2), but expected square deviation $35/12 \approx 2.9$ (the mean of the equally likely squared deviations 1/4, 9/4, and 25/4). As another example, the two roots of the quadratic $ax^2 + bx + c$ have mean the root of its derivative $2ax + b$, namely $x = -b/2a$, and Variance its discriminant $b^2 - 4ac$ divided by $4a^2$, this being the square deviation of each root from the mean.

Asian option — An Asian option (or average value option) is a special type of option contract. Fs the payoff is determined by the average underlying price over some pre-set period of time. This is different to the case of the usual European option and American option, where the payoff of the option contract depends on the price of the underlying instrument at maturity.

Chapter 16. Financing and Valuation

Barrier option	In finance, a Barrier option is a type of financial option where the option to exercise depends on the underlying crossing or reaching a given barrier level. Barrier options are always cheaper than a similar option without barrier. Barrier options were created to provide the insurance value of an option without charging as much premium.
Compound option	Compound option or split fee option is option on an option. The exercise payoff of a Compound option involves the value of another option. A Compound option then has two expiration dates and two strike prices.
Financial statements	financial statements (or financial reports) are formal records of the financial activities of a business, person, including United Kingdom company law, financial statements are often referred to as accounts, although the term financial statements is also used, particularly by accountants. financial statements provide an overview of a business or person"s financial condition in both short and long term.
New York Stock Exchange	The New York Stock Exchange is a stock exchange located at 11 Wall Street in lower Manhattan, New York City, New York, USA. It is the largest stock exchange in the world by United States dollar value of its listed companies" securities. As of October 2008, the combined capitalization of all domestic New York Stock Exchange listed companies was US$10.1 trillion. The New York Stock Exchange is operated by New York Stock Exchange Euronext, which was formed by the New York Stock Exchange "s 2007 merger with the fully-electronic stock exchange Euronext.
Stock exchange	A Stock exchange is a corporation or mutual organization which provides "trading" facilities for stock brokers and traders, to trade stocks and other securities. Stock exchanges also provide facilities for the issue and redemption of securities as well as other financial instruments and capital events including the payment of income and dividends. The securities traded on a Stock exchange include: shares issued by companies, unit trusts, derivatives, pooled investment products and bonds.
Stock split	A Stock split or stock divide increases or decreases the number of shares in a public company. The price is adjusted such that the market capitalization of the company remains the same after the split, so that dilution does not occur. Options and warrants are included.
Balance sheet	In financial accounting, a Balance sheet or statement of financial position is a summary of a person"s or organization"s balances. Assets, liabilities and ownership equity are listed as of a specific date, such as the end of its financial year. A Balance sheet is often described as a snapshot of a company"s financial condition.
Current asset	In accounting, a current asset is an asset on the balance sheet which is expected to be sold or otherwise used up in the near future, usually within one year, cash equivalents, accounts receivable, inventory, the portion of prepaid accounts which will be used within a year, and short-term investments. On the balance sheet, assets will typically be classified into current assets and long-term assets.
KPMG	International auditors KPMG were chosen by the Coalition Provisional Authority and the International Advisory and Monitoring Board to perform external audits of the Coalition"s expenditures from the humanitarian Development Fund for Iraq. The IAMB started negotiating with the CPA to appoint an external auditor in December 2003. KPMG was appointed in April 2004, to audit the CPA"s expenditures from Iraq"s oil revenue in 2003. United Nations Resolution 1483 transferred the authority to authorize expenditures from Iraq"s oil revenue from the United Nations to the Coalition Provisional Authority.

Chapter 16. Financing and Valuation

Chapter 16. Financing and Valuation

	It also created an international body to monitor the Coalition"s expenditures from Iraq"s oil revenue, the IAMB. The Coalition"s authority to expend Iraq"s oil revenue was conditional.
Working capital	working Capital is a financial metric which represents operating liquidity available to a business. Along with fixed assets such as plant and equipment, working Capital is considered a part of operating capital. It is calculated as current assets minus current liabilities.
Comprehensive income	Comprehensive income (or earnings) is a specific term used in companies" financial reporting from the company-whole point of view. Because that use excludes the effects of changing ownership interest, an economic measure of Comprehensive income is necessary for financial analysis from the shareholders" point of view
	Comprehensive income is defined by the Financial Accounting Standards Board, or FASB, as "the change in equity [net assets] of a business enterprise during a period from transactions and other events and circumstances from nonowner sources. It includes all changes in equity during a period except those resulting from investments by owners and distributions to owners."
	Comprehensive income is the sum of net income and other items that must bypass the income statement because they have not been realized, including items like an unrealized holding gain or loss from available for sale securities and foreign currency translation gains or losses.
Earnings before interest and taxes	In financial and business accounting, Earnings before interest and taxes (EBIT) or operating income is a measure of a firm"s profitability that excludes interest and income tax expenses.
	EBIT = Operating Revenue - Operating Expenses (OPEX) + Non-operating Income
	Operating Income = Operating Revenue - Operating Expenses
	Operating income is the difference between operating revenues and operating expenses, but it is also sometimes used as a synonym for EBIT and operating profit. This is true if the firm has no non-operating income.
Income statement	Income statement, also called profit and loss statement (P'L) and Statement of Operations, is a company"s financial statement that indicates how the revenue (money received from the sale of products and services before expenses are taken out, also known as the "top line") is transformed into the net income (the result after all revenues and expenses have been accounted for, also known as the "bottom line"). The purpose of the income statement is to show managers and investors whether the company made or lost money during the period being reported.
	The important thing to remember about an income statement is that it represents a period of time.
Market value	market value is the price at which an asset would trade in a competitive Walrasian auction setting. market value is often used interchangeably with open market value, fair value or fair market value, although these terms have distinct definitions in different standards, and may differ in some circumstances.
	International Valuation Standards defines market value as "the estimated amount for which a property should exchange on the date of valuation between a willing buyer and a willing seller in an arm"s-length transaction after proper marketing wherein the parties had each acted knowledgeably, prudently, and without compulsion."
	market value is a concept distinct from market price, which is "the price at which one can transact", while market value is "the true underlying value" according to theoretical standards.

Chapter 16. Financing and Valuation

Chapter 16. Financing and Valuation

Accounts receivable	Accounts receivable (A/R) is one of a series of accounting transactions dealing with the billing of customers who owe money to a person, company or organization for goods and services that have been provided to the customer. In most business entities this is typically done by generating an invoice and mailing or electronically delivering it to the customer, who in turn must pay it within an established timeframe called credit or payment terms. An example of a common payment term is Net 30, which means payment is due in the amount of the invoice 30 days from the date of invoice.
Asset	In business and accounting, Assets are economic resources owned by business or company. Anything tangible or intangible that one possesses, usually considered as applicable to the payment of one"s debts is considered an Asset. Simplistically stated, Assets are things of value that can be readily converted into cash (although cash itself is also considered an Asset).
Asset turnover	Asset turnover is a financial ratio that measures the efficiency of a company"s use of its assets in generating sales revenue or sales income to the company. $$Asset\ Turnover = \frac{Sales}{Average Total Assets}$$ · "Sales" is the value of "Net Sales" or "Sales" from the company"s income statement · "Average Total Assets" is the value of "Total assets" from the company"s balance sheet in the beginning and the end of the fiscal period divided by 2.
Average collection period	Receivable Turnover Ratio is one of the accounting liquidity ratios, a financial ratio. This ratio measures the number of times, on average, receivables (e.g. Accounts Receivable) are collected during the period. A popular variant of the receivables turnover ratio is to convert it into an Average collection period in terms of days.
Current ratio	The Current ratio is a financial ratio that measures whether or not a firm has enough resources to pay its debts over the next 12 months. It compares a firm"s current assets to its current liabilities. It is expressed as follows: $$Current\ ratio = \frac{Current\ Assets}{Current\ Liabilities}$$ For example, if WXY Company"s current assets are \$50,000,000 and its current liabilities are \$40,000,000, then its Current ratio would be \$50,000,000 divided by \$40,000,000, which equals 1.25. It means that for every dollar the company owes it has \$1.25 available in current assets.
Debt ratio	Debt ratio is a financial ratio that indicates the percentage of a company"s assets are provided via debt. It is the ratio of total debt (the sum of current liabilities and long-term liabilities) and total assets (the sum of current assets, fixed assets, and other assets such as "goodwill"). $$Debt\ ratio = \frac{Total\ Debt}{Total\ Assets}$$ or alternatively: $$Debt\ ratio = \frac{Total\ Liability}{Total\ Assets}$$ For example, a company with \$2 million in total assets and \$500,000 in total liabilities would have a Debt ratio of 25%

Chapter 16. Financing and Valuation

Chapter 16. Financing and Valuation

	Like all financial ratios, a company's Debt ratio should be compared with their industry average or other competing firms.
Dividend yield	The Dividend yield or the dividend-price ratio on a company stock is the company's annual dividend payments divided by its market cap
Efficiency ratio	The efficiency ratio, a ratio that is typically applied to banks, in simple terms is defined as expenses as a percentage of revenue (expenses / revenue), with a few variations. A lower percentage is better since that means expenses are low and earnings are high. It is related to operating leverage, which measures the ratio between fixed costs and variable costs.
Inventory	inventory is a list for goods and materials, held available in stock by a business. It is also used for a list of the contents of a household and for a list for testamentary purposes of the possessions of someone who has died. In accounting inventory is considered an asset.
Inventory turnover	The Inventory turnover is an equation that equals the cost of goods sold divided by the average inventory. Average inventory equals beginning inventory plus ending inventory divided by 2. The formula f: $$\text{Inventory Turnover} = \frac{\text{Cost of Goods Sold}}{\text{Average Inventory}}$$ The formula for average inventory: $$\text{Average Inventory} = \frac{\text{Beginning inventory} + \text{Ending inventory}}{2}$$ A low turnover rate may point to overstocking, obsolescence, or deficiencies in the product line or marketing effort. However, in some instances a low rate may be appropriate, such as where higher inventory levels occur in anticipation of rapidly rising prices or shortages.
Liquidity	Market liquidity is a business, economics or investment term that refers to an asset's ability to be easily converted through an act of buying or selling without causing a significant movement in the price and with minimum loss of value. Money, or cash on hand, is the most liquid asset. An act of exchange of a less liquid asset with a more liquid asset is called liquidation.
Net profit	In business and finance accounting, net profit is equal to the gross profit minus overheads minus interest payable plus/minus one off items for a given time period (usually: accounting period). A common synonym for "net profit" when discussing financial statements (which include a balance sheet and an income statement) is the bottom line. This term results from the traditional appearance of an income statement which shows all allocated revenues and expenses over a specified time period with the resulting summation on the bottom line of the report.
Net profit margin	Profit margin, net margin, Net profit margin or net profit ratio all refer to a measure of profitability. It is calculated by finding the net profit as a percentage of the revenue.

Chapter 16. Financing and Valuation

$$\text{Net profit margin} = \frac{\text{Net profit (after taxes)}}{\text{Revenue}} \times 100\%$$

The profit margin is mostly used for internal comparison.

Payout ratio

Dividend payout ratio is the fraction of net income a firm pays to its stockholders in dividends:

$$\text{Dividend payout ratio} = \frac{\text{Dividends}}{\text{Net Income for the same period}}$$

The part of the earnings not paid to investors is left for investment to provide for future earnings growth. Investors seeking high current income and limited capital growth prefer companies with high Dividend payout ratio. However investors seeking capital growth may prefer lower payout ratio because capital gains are taxed at a lower rate.

Quick

Quick is an electronic purse system available on Austrian bank cards to allow small purchases to be made without cash. The history of the Quick system goes back to 1994.

The system is aimed at small retailers such as bakeries, cafés, drink and parking automats (but even small discount shops such as Billa accept it) and intended for purchases of less than â,¬400. The card is inserted into a handheld Quick reader by the merchant who enters the transaction amount for the customer. The customer then confirms the purchase by pushing a button on the keypad, the exact amount debited from the card within a few seconds.

Quick ratio

$$\text{Quick (Acid Test) Ratio} = \frac{\text{Cash} + \text{Marketable Securities} + \text{Accounts Receivable}}{\text{Current Liabilities}}$$

Generally, the acid test ratio should be 1:1 or better, however this varies widely by industry. In general, the higher the ratio, the greater the company"s liquidity (i.e., the better able to meet current obligations using liquid assets).
Notice that very often Acid test refers instead of Quick ratio to Cash ratio:

$$\text{Acid Test Ratio} = \frac{\text{Cash} + \text{Marketable Securities}}{\text{Current Liabilities}}$$

Return on assets

The Return on assets percentage shows how profitable a company"s assets are in generating revenue.

Return on assets can be computed as:

$$\text{ROA} = \frac{\text{Net Income} + \text{Interest Expense} - \text{Interest Tax savings}}{\text{Average Total Assets}}$$

This number tells you what the company can do with what it has, i.e. how many dollars of earnings they derive from each dollar of assets they control. Its a useful number for comparing competing companies in the same industry.

Return on equity

Return on equity (Return on equity, Return on average common equity, return on net worth, Return on ordinary shareholders" funds) (requity) measures the rate of return on the ownership interest (shareholders" equity) of the common stock owners. It measures a firm"s efficiency at generating profits from every unit of shareholders" equity (also known as net assets or assets minus liabilities). Return on equity shows how well a company uses investment funds to generate earnings growth.

Chapter 16. Financing and Valuation

CPSIA information can be obtained
at www.ICGtesting.com
Printed in the USA
LVHW10s1203160818
587153LV00004B/46/P